I0441418

BUTTERFLY RENAISSANCE

A Self Help Recovery Novel
By Blaine MacNeil

butterflyrenaissance@live.com

TABLE OF CONTENTS

This book is dedicated to my beloved daughter.

Laura

BUTTERFLY RENAISSANCE
INTRODUCTION

This is the story of a society of butterflies who have their functional and dysfunctional sides. This particular 'species', as they refer to themselves, is plagued by dysfunction at so many levels in critical stages of development that they hardly resemble butterflies at all. Instead, they are more like the caterpillars who began but never finished the transformation of becoming a butterfly.

One member of this species resolves to overcome his inherited dysfunction and sets out to undo his past upbringing and make a new life for himself. Along the way he finds that this desire and resolve alone are not enough to dismantle and then rebuild his life. It's only due to friends he meets along the way who show him a better way of life and help him that he is able to help himself. Then he is able to work out his desire for a normal and healthy lifestyle.

Among the dysfunctional traits in his society is the assistance of the caterpillars out of their eggs and butterflies out of their cocoons. The society believes they are saving each other the torture and pain of a difficult and unnecessary task. This unfortunately leaves the butterflies with deformed wings that won't expand. Because of this they end up looking stunted and stubby with wings that are useless for flight. This society has developed the idea that flying is not something their species does. Besides this, the fabric of the cocoons are saved and rewoven into new clothes and used as building material for their houses and barns.

Trials beset the best efforts of this butterfly to change. In an attempt to fly he is publicly humiliated and seriously injured. At that point his family has no other choice but to ask for help from the flying butterflies who maybe can provide some help with recovery. Taken to a hospital in the flying butterfly's community, he works harder than he ever has before in his life and is able to recover with the skilled help of caring and healing therapists. He finds the help he could not give himself to rebuild the damage done to his body and learns to fly like butterflies were meant to.

BUTTERFLY RENAISSANCE
CHAPTER ONE
THE BIRTH OF DEWEY

In the spring of the year Marshall Branchwhalker and his wife Marge were excitedly busy with their many preparations for their coming happy event. Soon they would be the proud parents of another batch of caterpillars. They were diligently reinforcing their nest in the corner of their cocoon house to make it a more secure place than ever before. This would protect their new family members from harm.

There also was the spring cleaning to do, the winter food stores needed to be moved from the barn into the house. Fresh water needed to be gathered and a score of other details that could not be done soon enough.

When the eggs would finally arrive, it would take all of Marshall's and his wife's time and energy to look after their tiny, helpless young. There was the feeding and the cleaning. As the babies got only a little older, someone would have to constantly keep a close eye on those little ones, to protect them from wandering out of the nest and onto the branch.

Even though they were well experienced as parents, with three previous batches of eggs, they also knew what a difficult task it was and how awesome a responsibility they had on their hands. Marshall's sister-in-law, Aunt Savannah, would be helping as much as she could with the older caterpillars that were still living in their house. That was one major concern in their lives that they felt somewhat at ease about. Never the less, they found there was always something more to do or more plans to make.

Early one rainy morning Marshall was woken by his wife, who nervously said, "It's time for the little ones to be born!"

With that he got out of bed, made some tea for himself and sat quietly, waiting to see what would happen. His wife clumsily made her way over to the newly reinforced nest and soon, with great effort, the eggs were laid. The tired mother watched, guarding over the eggs and keeping them warm with the closeness of her body.

It wasn't long after this that the little ones could be heard pecking and poking from the inside of their hard little eggs. Soon the sound of cracking was added to the noisy clatter. With that, Marshall, who was now anxiously standing by, started to break open the eggs and pull out the caterpillars. He was very protective of his little babies and did not want the shells to bring injury or discomfort to even one of his newborn caterpillars.

After the last caterpillar was taken out of its shell, he set out fresh water and leaves. The leaves had been meticulously diced up into very small pieces, to make a salad that would be very easy for the babies to grasp and eat. When it was all over everyone was exhausted. The adults took turns, starting with Marshall, sleeping and keeping watch over the new baby caterpillars.

REBEL WITH A CAUSE

As the new batch of young ate and grew, they started to wander out from the nest that their parents had made for them in the corner of the house. This nest had been their only experience in life so far and they were quickly growing curious about the outside world. As soon as one caterpillar would creep out, Dad, Mom, or an older caterpillar that was standing by as a second in the line of defense, would scoop them up, pat their little bottoms and return them to the safety of the corner nest.

One particular new born was very much the rebel and he was constantly on the move. If he wasn't scampering about, he was climbing on top of the other caterpillars in the crowded nest in an attempt to boost himself out. It was as though he was trying to break the record for attempts to get out the front door.

Marshall commented to everyone, "Keep an awful close eye on this fast little one. I have no idea why he is so bent on getting out of the nest at such a young age. But, if he's so determined to get out, with as good as he's got it, being hand fed and served, it must be a bad sign. He just doesn't know how good he's got it."

Well, it really wasn't long and sure enough that little one did get out of the corner nest again. He scampered quickly across the floor, in and out of everyone's grasp and then out through the entryway of the house. Everyone took off after him. What a day this was to remember.

When they got out the door they could see him going the wrong direction on the branch, not up or down, but to the side and to the edge. Marshall ran with all his might toward the wayward son, calling and coaxing him not to go on. None the less, this fearless little one just kept right on going until it was too late.

Marshall could not get to him in time and the baby started to slip off the edge of the branch. This didn't seem to scare the young caterpillar into stopping or turning around, he just seemed to have a natural fearlessness about him. Marshall was frantic when he saw the little one walk off the edge and fall to the ground far below. He quickly turned around, running as fast as he could to the main central branch that led to the trunk of their tree and swiftly made his way down. Right behind him were some older caterpillars. As they approached the ground, they became quiet, thinking to themselves, that he would surely be dead. But no one would admit it aloud, no one dared. It was to everyone's delight to see that as Marshall reached him, this young rebel was found alive and well, and trying to get his bearings on the tall, wet spring grass he had fallen onto.

Marshall proclaimed, "It's impossible, he's alive and he's not even hurt!" He noticed a patch of terrible thistles just inches away from his son. He was so grateful he didn't fall into them or get one stuck on himself. They were very difficult to remove at the very least and sometimes they even impossible to remove. He picked him up while wiping off the morning dew that was dripping from this little one's forehead and said, "We will call you Dewey, because I found you covered in the morning dew."

Then they all made their way back up the tree to the house. The rest of the family was wallowing in tears, fully expecting the men to be bringing back a dead young caterpillar. As the rescue team approached they shouted with great joy that "The baby's OKAY!" This not only surprised everyone still at the house, but it took them a moment to get used to the idea as well. The mother could hardly believe her ears and so she ran to see if it was true. She took the little one into her arms and held him tightly, rocking him gently. Sobbing and stroking her baby's antennas, as she said, "I'll never let this happen to you again, never. We should have watched you more closely."

UNDER A WATCHFUL EYE

Dewey's early journey from his nest and eventful fall from his family's branch was not a lesson this family was about to forget. The family took turns watching Dewey closely after this. No matter what he was doing, he did not do it without a watchful set of eyes on him from an older brother or sister standing near by. This gave Dewey a chance to be tutored by his older and more educated siblings, who always tried to explain life to him. The family hoped that they could teach him just some sensibility, to prevent him from crashing off the side of a branch again, or doing something else even more foolish. Any question he had was instantly answered and anything he had need of was instantly provided for him by a very willing and protective family, who cared for him in his youth both night and day.

Dewey's favorite sister, Beverly, was also, very fond of Dewey. She enjoyed the role of taking care of Dewey a great deal and hoped that all the time she invested in this would some day make her a good mother.

Dewey questioned her one day, saying, "Bev, why do things fall to the ground below? What makes this happen?"

Bev, not sure of what to say, answered without hesitation anyway, saying, "Things fall because ... uh, they fall to the ground because they have no one to hold them up. Without help they are bound to go down."

"But, Bev, what is it that makes them go down instead of sideways or up?"

"They don't go up because the mocking birds might get them then. They don't go sideways because you can't fall sideways, you have to slip in order to go that direction."

Dewey was pleased with all the many answers he had acquired from his brothers and sisters. The information filled his mind and kept him from wondering on his own too much. He hoped one day he could acquire enough knowledge so that all he learned would come together into one large picture with some kind of consistency to it.

One of Dewey's brothers, Ed, was also among those whose influence he highly regarded. Ed was a caterpillar that had completed his cocoon class training but stayed around home a bit longer than was typical of caterpillars. Dewey posed questions to him that he felt could not be answered well by any one else, if they could be answered at all. Dewey asked him one day, "Is knowledge limited or without limits?"

Ed shook his head and said, "That is a good question, but where did you come up with it?"

"I don't know, but it seems that everyone has an answer to everything and that very little is left unaccounted for.", Dewey responded.

Ed thought for quite a while and then said, "You're right about accountability and our society. But as far as knowledge in our society, whether it is limited in its volume or not is of little consequence. What matters is that we cannot, as individuals, know it all and as a society, even if we know a great deal, it would still not be the thing that cures our ills."

Dewey was silent for a moment and then thanked Ed for his answer even though he did not fully understand it. Then again, he wasn't even sure he understood his own question very well. However, Dewey did have a mind for details and remembered things well. He hoped that all this attention and guidance his family gave him would boost his performance when it came time for him to go to school. He would be old enough for cocoon classes very soon.

THE ATTACK OF THE MOCKING BIRDS

It was a miserably day. The young caterpillars were told not to wander far from the cocoon house, but not why. Dewey's father worrying that the food wouldn't last long, commented, "The rain is too infrequent."

Dewey questioned him, "Dad, how much is enough?"

"More is enough, this is too little." Marshall snapped.

Dewey felt unhappy with the answer and thought maybe his father had no idea of how much was enough. But then, no one else seemed to know either or at least they weren't saying it if they did know. At any rate, Dewey had learned that if he asked too many questions in a row of his father he would anger him. So he kept the rest of his thoughts to himself.

Marshall went down the tree trunk to the ground below to scout around even though he had forbidden his family to do this. Dewey could see him eating the leaves of grass and scraping the ground. Marshall looked up to the sky and then to the horizon, as though searching the distance for something. As he started back up the tree trunk it was clear to see that he was in a hurry. When he got back, he had his entire family stay in the house for the rest of the day. This continued for several days. Then he started going over to the neighbor's houses for meetings. He and his wife talked in hushed voices saying nothing to the rest of the family about what was going on.

One quiet day everyone was in the house and bored. All of a sudden Dewey saw a large shadow pass quickly over the house. It was accompanied by a noise sounding like the wind ruffling the leaves, but it was strangely different.

Dewey's mom looked worried and his father looked angry. They quickly rushed the family together in a huddle and in stern voices told everyone to be very quiet. "What a bother!" Dewey thought, as it happened again. Only now, something seemed to hit the house and pull at it. A hole appeared in the roof and Dewey saw something black move swiftly by. He wasn't worried much, but his mom sure was. Then something came and landed right on their branch, in full view in front of the door. Darkness covered the house from their out-stretched wings and Dewey could see it was the mocking birds attacking.

Many of the birds went to the cocoon barn and tore away pieces of it trying to poke their large heads in to get to the food, but they were not successful. The ones at the house flapped their wings and made shrilling noises. They tore bits and pieces of the cocoon fabric off the frame of the house and turned their heads sideways to look inside.

One stuck his little beak in the hole and snapped at them. He got a hold of the mom's antenna and she screamed at first. Then she said "It doesn't hurt!" So after he let go she poked at the bird's eye with her antenna and got him good. Dewey's dad warned her not to anger the birds further. You could see how Dewey's mom was glad she had been able to injure the bird for the terror he was bringing to their house. But, in her carelessness, she got too close to the hole in the house again and the bird stuck his beak in and this time bit down hard on her antenna. She looked surprised and wailed in pain and wiggled to get free. The bird seemed to know he had hurt her back and so let her go. Dewey's mom collapsed to the floor, crying quietly and curling up into a ball. Then the mocking birds flew off.

Marshall sent two of the older caterpillars to get help from one of the cocoonmums. They are social matriarchs that provide for such things as care when a butterfly is injured. He hoped one would come and help by doing something to ease his wife's pain. Soon a cocoonmum arrived and took a look at her.

Shaking her head the cocoonmum said, "Tisk, tisk, tisk. What has happened to you and what can I do here? Can I offer you some help?"

As his mom told her story, the cocoonmum opened her sack made of cocoon fabric, pulled out some oily smelly balm and wiped it on the painful antenna. Then she wrapped the antenna in a cocoon fabric dressing and added some ridged splints made from young small branches, to hold it upright. After his mom was done telling her story, the cocoonmum explained that the antenna in their species of butterfly are not very sensitive on the outside. That was why the mother didn't feel any pain when the mocking bird first bit her.

But, the cocoonmum added, that underneath the insensitive surface, the antenna are especially sensitive, to an extreme. The second time the bird bit harder and was able to penetrate the insensitive surface, down to the core of the antenna, where the pain level is great.

The cocoomum said she would return daily to change the dressings and check on Dewey's mom's progress. She did return daily for about two weeks until the wound on the antenna was completely healed over. One thing though, not only did the painful sensitivity of the antenna go away, but so did her ability to be sensitive to many other things too.

BUTTERFLY RENAISSANCE
CHAPTER TWO
COCOON CLASS DAZE

Though butterflies' families are large, they still try to give each and every young caterpillar more special attention than the next, in order to help get them off on the right foot in life. They had learned over the generations that careful attention needed to be given to the upbringing of their young. This would ensure that all future generations would follow in the accomplishments that had already been achieved.

No one wanted to go backwards into the previous failures that had threatened their species. For instance, once, maybe more than once, their population had gotten so large that they overwhelmed the productivity of the tree their society lived on. The supplies of leaves and nectar could not keep up with the many young caterpillars and butterflies that tried to live on this one tree. As a result, many starved, others continually fought for territory and many left never to be heard from again.

Those who remained and survived developed ways to keep their society orderly. They reasoned that they must never again overwhelm the tree's ability to produce food for everyone, so no one would ever need to leave again. The butterflies knew that with weather changes, food would not always grow in abundance. So they stored up large amounts of food for these times, to prevent the need to go elsewhere as many had in generations past. The society developed unwritten codes for many of their values and practices especially for the control of branches, so that your branch would be respected and not harvested by anyone else.

To ensure the transition of their society's values and way of life to every caterpillar born to their society they developed cocoon classes. All the families saw to it that every caterpillar went. The caterpillars went because they were told it was their gateway to adulthood and because they had no choice.

Cocoon classes were held in the Great Hollow of the Tree. This was in the main stem of the trees branches. It was a large, deep opening that had been there longer than anyone could remember. Even the oldest of the society's members had no idea how it came to exist, no memory of so much as a story or legend of its origin. Some butterflies speculated it was there before the species came to inhabit the tree, but no one could verify this. Just inside the opening there was a large area, with a low ceiling. It was very wide, wide enough for butterflies to gather in, with a smooth flat floor. This area was used by the society for large meetings, the festivals and cocoon classes. Farther back though, the hollow narrowed, so much so a butterfly or caterpillar could not turn around to get out. No one ever ventured this far in.

DAY ONE

On this particular day all of the young caterpillars had gathered together in the Great Hollow and were sitting in a circle anxious for their first day of class to begin. Many nervously fidgeted in place while waiting for one of the cocoonmums to arrive and get things going. They had all been instructed by their parents on what to expect and how to behave; to sit still, listen attentively and not to disrupt.

As they talked among themselves a rather large and elderly butterfly entered the circle and spoke out. "Hello, and good morning. I'm Cocoonmum Hasselmeyer and I will be one of your instructors here in cocoon class. We have a lot of material to cover so I will simply ask you to hold all of your questioning until the end so we don't fall behind. Your questions may be answered during the lectures anyway." Then the cocoonmum turned and looked everyone over, head to tail, giving extra time to a few in the class.

"With that said, I will start today's lesson. The subject is our cocoons, which you will all be spinning shortly after graduation.

"More generations ago than we can number the cocoon was simply discarded and left to the elements of the weather to rot away after the butterfly came out.

However, for as long as I can remember and then some, our society has found it is actually of great value and useful for servicing our needs. For instance, as you have undoubtedly noticed, it has been servicing all adults in our society for such important things as clothing, housing and storage barns, to name just a few of the most obvious benefits we are enjoying."

As Dewey sat, watching and listening, just as his parents had instructed him to do, his concentration was suddenly and rudely interrupted by his friend, Thomas, who, with a hard twist, pinched him in the arm. He was told by his friend it was a game and that he should pass it on to the person next to him. Dewey, not happy to be distracted from what the cocoonmum was saying and knowing this game was not allowed, simply tried to pinch Thomas back. The cocoonmum might not have noticed, or if she had noticed, she might not have said anything, but Thomas moved quickly to get far from Dewey's reach.

The Cocoonmum quickly spoke out in anger, "Dewey, I don't care what has been going on, or who started it but you know without being told that pinching games are simply not allowed. You are disturbing my class and wasting everyone's valuable time. This is the first, last and only warning I will give to you. Do not cross me!"

Dewey's heart sank deep and his anger welled up inside. He was mad at Thomas for playing that stupid pinching game and for pinching so hard. Dewey was mad that the cocoonmum had yelled only at him and didn't care to find out that at least one other person was involved in it. Dewey worried that the cocoonmum might speak to his parents and get him in trouble at home. He felt doubly wronged that none of it was right. He sat in class with his head held low and rehearsed repeatedly how wrong the whole thing was.

The cocoonmum returned to her lesson. "We have found that the fabric, when correctly handled and properly treated will last and last. It will last for at least three and up to four generations of use, wear, tear and even abuse. If it is left to itself though, it will rot away in no time at all. So by saving the cocoon and using its fabric, we can extend its usefulness beyond the temporary shelter it was originally used for during the changes we start to go through from adolescence to adulthood.

"In order to extend its usefulness we must, at times, attempt to repair the wear and tear that occurs. The cocoon fabric can be repaired with the use of new cocoon fabric, by cutting a patch to fit and weaving it on with a needle and thread.

"Because of the long life of the fabric we can pass it on to our descendants generation after generation. You will find, after you graduate, your first cocoon clothes will be made from cocoon fabric that was one of your ancestor's and now is passed on to you, as part of your inheritance. Later your own cocoon will be, with the addition of your ancestors cocoon fabric, woven into additional clothes, housing and storage barns.

"Our society has developed these practices for many different reasons. Because we are an advanced and civilized species of butterfly, we choose to do what no other species does and wear our cocoons as clothing. We must keep up our appearances, so we don't look inferior. We know that if we look our best at all times, others will like us and things will go well for us.

"Well, it looks like we've gone over our time limit and so why don't we stop here. We'll pick up tomorrow where we left off. Class is dismissed."

Dewey didn't want to wait around to answer questions the other caterpillars would have about why he got yelled at. He also was certain he didn't want to talk with his friend Thomas, who had gotten him in big trouble. So he headed straight out of the classroom and to his home. There he sat and thought about how to not get caught when he was getting into trouble next time.

DAY TWO

The next day of class all the young caterpillars gathered for cocoon class. The morning was bright and sunny and it was starting to warm up quickly. Most of the caterpillars had been up working late into the night. Many yawned, looking very dreary and sleepy-eyed. In fact, a few were nodding off, only to be awakened by the cocoonmum who was not very happy. To her it was not OKAY to be sleepy.

She spoke out loudly, "Good morning class, I will not have my students drifting off and inattentive in front of me. Everybody wake up and stay that way!"

The entire class immediately sat up straight and at attention. Those who had been sleeping and were caught off guard had no idea what had happened until a few moments had passed and they got their bearings again.

"That's better. Now, if you're done chasing your dreams and sleeping when you shouldn't be, we will get started. I'm Cocoonmum Benntwhing and today I'm your teacher. We're going to cover the lesson on cocoon spinning and birthing process. You will find instinctively that spinning a cocoon is no problem for you. I think by now, in your short little lives, you must have seen someone spin a cocoon. But, just to review what you must already know I will go over it with you again. The thing I must emphasize most of all is that you want to make the absolute best, finely spun, high quality cocoon possible. Remember that not only will you wear it for a life time, but so will your children, their children and possibly their children too. That makes three to four generations of use for the cocoon fabric.

"Now the first thing that you do is to start a thread and spin a belt and strap it around your hind most feet and then you attach them to the tree branch along with your tail. Then you continue to spin and weave your fabric, working your way up toward your waist, back and forth in repetition. Don't let yourselves be distracted by anyone, and I mean anyone! Once the process has begun it is critical that no one helps or distracts you from your work.

"At the waist, you add one more special strap, like a belt again and string it around, attaching yourself to the cocoon a second time. Then, continuing to weave back and forth, sideways and up and down, closing your self in.

"Eventually, you will start to close the area around your head and things will go very dark, as the sun light begins to be blocked out. This, you might think would cause you some uneasiness, but you will be amazed at what you actually feel. The snugness of the cocoon along with a special sense of accomplishment begins to over take you. This is enhanced by a real sense of pre-emergence into an adult butterfly. There will be nothing else like it, ever again in your life time, nor can this process ever be repeated. So that is why we place so much emphasis on the importance of these events.

"Because of this tremendous feeling of impending potential change and other reasons too, we wear our cocoon clothes as adults to continually remind us of this time in our lives. It is a feeling we want to keep familiar to us forever.

"Inside the cocoon, changes start to take place in you. You are in the process of becoming a butterfly after the species of butterfly that all your ancestors were, a non-flying one. Remember what I now say, *WE ARE SPECIAL, WE ARE UNLIKE NO OTHER*! It's important that you remember I said that to you.

"In the cocoon you will be in a sleep-like state. When you awaken you will obviously need help to get out of the cocoon. You must have the help of a cocoonmum. So you don't destroy the fabric's continuity or get physically damaged yourselves in trying to get out.

"The cocoonmums have been taught that the flying species of butterflies have no help in getting free of their cocoons. As a result of this they must wreck their cocoon in escaping, leaving it ruined because they stretched it to the point of breaking. They themselves are in a great deal of danger; suffering pain, physical and emotional stress and could die in the process. We know, from experience, that if you help a flying species of butterfly out of its cocoon, it will die.

"In our society, however, we are much more caring, taking into consideration the caterpillar and saving you from great danger. This is most certainly a process that you should not have to do alone. We will not let our young and inexperienced members suffer this way. The cocoonmums have the knowledge and training to both properly preserve the cocoon and get you out safely. We use ceremonial instruments to cut the cocoon open, avoiding the possibility of you getting hurt or even dying.

"So when you wake up from your sleep, don't forget to call out for help. Calling out for help seems to be less than instinctive, so I will repeat, don't forget this. Call out for help. Then a family member who is sitting vigil for you will go and get the cocoonmum and your family. When the cocoonmum arrives she will call out your name to assure it is you and that you are ready. Answer correctly with your name, then she will cut you free. Be sure to hold very still, the less struggling you do the better.

"It seems to be almost instinctive to move and wiggle like a worm, but we are not worms, so don't embarrass your family, don't wiggle. Be sure to hold very still, so you don't accidentally get cut.

"When the cocoonmum is done, she will pull you out and dry you off, because you will be wet. Then you will have your cocoon robe put on you and the cocoonmum will present you to your family and friends giving you your full name."

"Cocoonmum, can I ask a question?" said Dewey, "Why are we wet, what purpose does it serve?".

"Well, Dewey, I see that you asked permission to ask a question, but you must also wait for permission to be granted before you ask the question. And don't forget to raise your hand into the air prior to that so I can decide if I will call on you or not. Anyway, why ... are we wet? No one has ever asked that question before. I think that the water serves no purpose at all. I think that's everything I wanted to say on today's topic, so class is dismissed."

DAY THREE

The next morning all the young caterpillars gathered again and sat in anticipation of another day. The cocoonmum came in and started the lesson.

"Today we are going to cover miscellaneous issues regarding our history, heritage and culture. We will also take a comparative look at non-flying and flying varieties of animal and insects.

"Some of the cultural values we hold are very closely tied in with our past. Historically, there was a time in our ancestor's lives when they ran out of food to eat. We don't really know why this happened, but we do know that many butterflies went hungry as a result of this. Some died and others left our tree never to be seen or heard of again. Basically our society crashed.

"So our ancestors devised ways to avoid another crash. We 'harvest' our food and we wait until the prime time to do this. Then we store our food in barns that we have built from cocoon fabric. By storing the food we will always have enough to eat for a very long time to come. This way we don't need to worry about food, except only ... mum...   well, maybe just a little. But while we do not worry about what we will eat today, tomorrow or the next day, or even beyond that, we must constantly remind ourselves to be occupying our minds with related issues. These are the basic ideas we hold about our species and why we are this way.   But, more on this later in another class on farming.

"Now to move on to the second half of the lesson, let's look at us as compared to those flying species of butterfly. First, let me introduce some well-known and undisputed facts of life. In the family of birds there are flying and non-flying types, the eagle and sparrow fly. On the other hand, the chicken does not fly and while the wild turkey can fly if it chooses too, the domestic turkey does not fly. The wild turkey was been inbred for centuries and by continual refinement and improvements, it simply does not fly any more. In the same way, some butterflies do not fly and some do fly. In our society we must take pride because we are civilized. Examples of this would be our advancements in our cocoon clothes, cocoon houses and our ability to hibernate when it comes to bad weather or attacks of the mocking birds. Additionally, we have our cocoon storage barns and cocoon art. We store food so we hopefully never run out again. We are settled and our society is very stable. As a society we don't change much, if at all.

"We don't view the flying species of butterfly as settled. Those butterflies don't harvest food to store, or save their cocoon fabric for good use and they have no permanent home. As a result of this they must go searching everyday for food. They must fly many, many miles to warm weather to avoid winter. Then they must fly back again, just as many miles, to where they started from in the first place. It is so silly, if you think about it for a moment. Who knows what they might find so many miles from here, it could be disastrous.

"Because they do fly, they can be easily attacked by the mocking birds not only in trees like us, they can also be attacked in the air, unlike us and then crash. This to me is just asking for trouble. With their bright colors and high profile, I imagine they must actually attract and appear to welcome being attacked. We can run to safety and hide in the secure feelings of our cocoon houses.

"Beyond these most obvious faults with their lifestyle, their egg birth and cocoon birth process is quite primitive. They don't help their little babies break out of the eggs or help with the even more difficult and dangerous cocoon birth.   Their young must risk hazards and I imagine suffer immensely to break free of their cocoons without help from anyone, let alone a cocoonmum.

"We work hard to keep our society running smoothly and to avoid these unnecessary hardships. Yet they seem to ride the winds and take their chances. However, we alone have a secure, unchanging way of life.

"OK, thanks for listening so well today. We seem to have gone over our time again, so I will let you all go now, bye."

The little caterpillars shuffled out one after the other. They were happy to get out of cocoon class so they could stretch their legs and use their voices.

DAY FOUR

On the next day of class the cocoonmum came late. She looked rushed and like she was expecting the class to be misbehaving. But all she could see were young caterpillars waiting for her to arrive and start the daily lesson.

"Today, young ones, we will take a panoramic view of the 'Cycle of Life', in our society. Basically, we will see how we repeat many actual or similar events throughout our life time.

"You know how we are naturally first an egg. This compares to our cocoon and the cocoon compares to the egg. Likewise just as your parents safely helped you with your egg birth, so also the cocoon birth is helped by the cocoonmum. Equally well, when we were caterpillars after the egg birth we are butterflies after the cocoon birth, we even look similar. This is why we call it a cycle, because of the identical or similar events and states that occur over and over again during our life times.

"None of you however, being less than one year old, knows or has lived through all of the four seasons that come each year. Spring, the season we are in now, is a time of awakening, the weather grows warm and the plants come to life. All of you were born in the spring, which is common for caterpillars. Summer, the next season, has very warm weather, a lot of sunshine and all the leaves grow large. In the fall, which is next, when things cool down, the final harvest takes place for late ripening plants. The leaves remaining on our tree will fall to the ground if we don't work hard enough to harvest them first. Lastly, winter comes, when it grows very cold, snow falls and we go into hibernation. Then spring returns and the four seasons cycle through again, and so on and so forth. This is another cycle of life.

"We also view the use of the cocoon fabric as a cycle, because it may last for up to three or four generations and can be rewoven and patched. Your great-grandparents could have worn the one you or one of your siblings may soon wear. Also, your children, grandchildren and your great-grandchildren could wear the cocoon you will weave.

"Can anyone think of another cycle?"

Dewey quickly remarked, "I remember when I was first learning to walk and I fell, crashing to the floor of my nest, but my father picked me up. Then I remember when I fell off our branch and I crashed to the ground below, but my family rescued me. Again, last night I fell when I was running and I crashed to the ground below me, but my friends picked me up. Is this an example of learning in a cycle, until you learn it the lesson keeps coming back?"

The cocoonmum looked impatient as she shook her head from side to side and simply said, "No. Is there anyone who has another example?"

Courtlynn, a petite caterpillar who was normally very quiet, surprised everyone by speaking up saying, "I have a question. I don't get it. Which way does the cycle go up or down?"

Everyone in the class instantly opened up into a rip roaring laugh.

Then the cocoonmum spoke out, "Quiet down now, or else I will have to speak to your parents!"

Everyone went immediately silent. The cocoonmum continued, "Courtlynn, the cycle is circular, like a wheel. The cycle doesn't go up or anything, it just goes round and round, over and over."

Courtlynn asked, "Then are we stuck on it?"

Almost everyone snickered under their breath. They felt this was not only a stupid question, but it was even more stupid than the first one. How did she dare to ask another one, especially after being laughed at for her first question?

The Cocoonmum responded, "No, we just repeat it over and over."

Then she continued with her lesson, "Because of these cycles we have learned it is better to follow our routines and habits that fit into the cycles very well. That way we tend to follow a course of less resistance. This reduces the stress of life that probably drove us to crashing as a society in the first place and made some butterflies leave us, never to be heard of again.

"Well, I think that is enough for you to listen to today. Class is dismissed."

Later that day, Marshall, Dewey's father, approached him and stated, "Dewey, I had a little visit from the cocoonmum today. She is not very happy with you right now and neither am I. She tells me that since cocoon classes started you have been disturbing the class, pinching others ..."

"But ... but ..." Dewey tried to speak in his own defense but his father would not be interrupted, "... asking questions out of turn and without permission ..."

Dewey tried to speak out again, "... but, ... well ... "

Marshall just continued, " ... and making irrelevant comments that take up class time. I'm not very pleased that the cocoonmum has to come over here and talk to me about your misbehaving. She is a very busy and important person. She should not have to put up with this. She said that it was you together with Courtlynn, who have been taking up much of her time.

"She also said she wonders if you have special needs because you might have suffered some brain damage when you fell off the tree as a youngster. Anyway, I don't want you making any more trouble in class for me, so keep your mouth shut and your hands to yourself."

Dewey had long since given up trying to explain to his father what his side of the story was. He felt humiliated and didn't care anymore. He just hoped this part of his life would be over soon so he could move out on his own.

DAY FIVE

The next day at cocoon class everyone showed that they pretty much knew the routine now. They showed up before the cocoonmum, sat quietly and said nothing. They all knew the cocoonmums would never let you forget it if you misbehaved or even said anything in their class.

"Good morning class." said the cocoonmum as she walked in, starting the early morning's lesson. "Today we have a guest speaker who will be sharing with us. Please welcome Audrey Budsman, who will be talking about her personal experiences as a member of our society and as a matriarch who has raised many of our fellow members. I will be supervising."

The cocoonmum sat down, then the speaker got up. She looked the class over, looked back at the cocoonmum and then she spoke. "I'm glad to be here and was delighted to be called upon to talk about myself regarding what life has been like as a butterfly in our society. As I thought about what I might like to say many things came to my mind. I had to spend a lot of time sorting through what I thought might be of value and of interest to you. I've found that in my life I have many fun memories. But instead, I decided that I would talk about my life when I was a young caterpillar, like you. What I was taught then has really stayed with me through the years. It is the pattern that I have had to live by. This was especially true when it came to raising my children.

"As a caterpillar, my parents felt cocoon class was important and so they brought me there to learn, just as they in turn had been brought by their parents and just as your parents are now bringing you. Everyday there was class I found myself sitting and learning, just as you are now. When I had children I also was compelled to bring them to cocoon class, as I myself had been.

"I never really questioned my parents. I was brought willingly, and my children similarly came because this was expected of them. I cannot imagine not having come. It was just the thing you do, very naturally.

"My faithfulness to this, in turn, made it easier when it came to raising my children. They accepted coming to cocoon class willingly, as I had. Whenever they might question me if it was really important to go, I just said, 'Yes, you're right. It is not only important, but is, in fact, really important!' That way they understood without it really being explained, that this is the thing to do. So, just as generations before, we would continue to honor this age-old and time-tested tradition.

"So, I developed this habit as a young caterpillar, benefiting from my parents fine example and as you can see it is also a lesson I have passed on. This is done in such a way in our family that it is given to every successive generation as well. Now as a grandparent I am able to supervise and ensure my children follow in these steps with their children.

"It is a way of perpetuating the lifestyle. Because of the natural outcome, it is sure to stay securely that way for up to three or perhaps four generations because of my influence alone. As I recall my youth, that is what I was taught as being the most important thing of all, so as to not lose all the progress we have achieved.".

The cocoonmum went to the front of the class and thanked Mrs. Budsman for her sharing with the class exactly as she was asked. Then, after Mrs. Budsman had left, the cocoonmum dismissed the class.

DISSONANCE OFF THE TREE

Dewey walked home slowly from cocoon class feeling unsure of himself and confused. He still felt a cloud over his head because of his father's lecture to him about not questioning the cocoonmum anymore. He didn't like being included with Courtlynn in this. He felt she was the one who had a brain injury, with her crazy remarks and the way everyone laughed at her.

He stopped walking for a lack of motivation and wondered what to do next. He wandered down off the tree that was his home and on to the ground below. There he sat down next to a puddle and stared into it. Across the surface of the water on the right he saw a very inviting view of the sky, its white clouds and the bright sun in the middle. Then he shifted to the left and saw his tree with its many branches. Then he moved to the middle this time and looked straight down. He saw himself!

Though he knew how a caterpillar looks, he had never considered how he looked. So he concentrated hard on his reflection and committed it to memory. Then a leaf floated down and landed in the puddle, sending waves and ripples across the surface of the water distorting his reflection. He waited for the water to settle down again, but all he could see now was the mud and debris on the bottom of the puddle.

He felt hungry and alone so he mustered up his willpower and slowly headed up the tree to his branch. When he arrived home, his mother remarked on his lateness. He did not want to open up to her about his feelings. He didn't want to tell her about not coming straight home as he was supposed to, or about getting off the tree like he is not supposed to at his young age.

So he simply said, "I walked slowly all the way home."

Dewey's mother said to him, "You will never be a very productive butterfly if you do everything this slowly."

Dewey just sat quietly and waited for lunch.

DAY SIX

The last day of cocoon class was finally here and all of the caterpillars sat anxiously waiting for what would come next. The morning was bright and energy filled the air as the cocoonmum entered the great hollow.

"Morning class, today we again have a lot to cover. We have a guest speaker, Earl Leafson, our agriculture instructor, who will give us a briefing on farming."

Earl stood up and walked to the front of the classroom. He cleared his throat thoroughly and stared as if he were blind the entire time he spoke. "I've been farming all of my life and have learned many things that have helped me be productive on my branch. I think I will start at the final steps and work my way backwards through the process of productive farming. It seems to be easier to do and makes more sense to me by explaining things this way.

"You know that most of the food we eat comes out of our cocoon storage barns. You must take the oldest food out first and eat it. That way you don't age the food any longer than necessary. When you store the food you have to do a lot of rearranging. Make sure the newer food is stored in the back of the barn and then move it forward in the order of its age, so the oldest food is eaten first.

"When it comes to harvesting food, we must wait for the prime time, when the food is ripe. Prior to this, the leaves and nectar taste too strong. You would not enjoy the flavor. Some food ripens early in the season, which is what you see at the midsummer harvest. The rest of the food ripens at the end of the summer and early in the fall. You must pull the leaf free of its branch or stock and move it to storage. The nectar, you squeeze and press from the flowers and store in vats made of cocoon fabric and nut shells.

"Prior to this, in the spring you will see the buds for leaves and flowers sprouting out. It is important that you do not eat these. Otherwise they will never mature and develop for use as food. One thing though, in an emergency you may eat some of these to survive, but not for any other purpose. That's about it. Thanks for listening." With that Earl left and the cocoonmum dismissed the class.

FINAL GRADES

After cocoon classes ended all the young caterpillars went home to wait impatiently for their final reports regarding their status. These would be given by the cocoonmums. They would give the report to the parents directly and then the parents would tell the young caterpillars.

A few days after cocoon classes had ended a cocoonmum showed up at Dewey's house and met privately with Dewey's parents. They met for about twenty minutes, which was longer than typical and this caused Dewey to worry excessively. The cocoonmum left hastily saying she had many parents to still meet with. After this, his parents came and met with him and reviewed what the cocoonmum had told them. Dewey was not surprised that he was downgraded for not living up to his potential, but did pass. Dewey could not remember anyone not ever passing.

The cocoonmum, his parents said, was critical of him for his strange questions. But, what really did surprise him was that he still managed to finish second to the top in his class. He wondered, if he had simply kept his comments and questions to himself, could he have been the best? But, it was too late for that now.

BUTTERFLY RENAISSANCE
CHAPTER THREE
REBIRTH AS A BUTTERFLY

Dewey's older siblings were now at that stage in their young lives to begin their cocoon spinning. They had completed all of their cocoon class training in the spring and the many preparations were completed for their emerging into adult life as flightless butterflies. Their cocoon robes and clothes were made.

Their inheritance of the food stores and other items, deemed necessary for their success in life, had been set aside. On the family branch they each set out when they felt they were ready and hung themselves upside down by their tails on the tree.

BEV'S COCOON BIRTH

Dewey watched his older sister, Bev, from a distance. She worked hard for many hours to spin and weave her cocoon, ignoring everything and everyone that was around her. With all seriousness she went about her careful work to insure that only a high quality, very finely spun and woven cocoon would result. She had such a detailed mind for these things. Dewey waved to her as she came close to closing herself in. Bev would not let herself notice. The cocoon wiggled a few times as she made her final touches on the inside for the changes she hoped to undergo shortly.

Dewey continued to watch for a little while and then sadly went home when a sibling came to take the watch. Though young, he had begun to understand that his relationship with his sister would never again be the same. Sometime soon she would call out and they would send for the cocoonmum. Then his sister would be delivered a new adult flightless butterfly who would go off, get married and have her own family. He would miss seeing her everyday, having her around to talk with and to help him with all the daily tasks in life. He realized now how much she had been like a mother to him, taking charge of so many things.

Time went by and as Dewey was starting his morning watch he heard his sister call out saying, "Hello, can you hear me? Is anyone out there?"

Dewey answered with all haste, "Bev, is that you? Are you awake now?"

"Yes!" she answered. "I'm awake and I'm ready. Would you please let Dad and Mom know and then could you go yourself and get a cocoonmum to come and birth me?"

Dewey felt so excited that he could hardly wait. He answered quickly, "Of course I will!" With that he was off, as fast as a caterpillar could go, to speak to their parents and then to run to a cocoonmum's house to bring her back.

Dewey's parents, nervous about all the things that could go wrong, gathered the family together at the branch where Bev had made her cocoon. Soon a cocoonmum came. Right behind her was Dewey, who was beginning to look a little tired from all the running around he had to do. The cocoonmum approached the cocoon and called out Bev's name to insure that she was awake and ready to come out.

Bev responded saying, "Oh, yes most certainly and if you don't mind I'm not just ready, I'm in a hurry. It's tight in here and I'm not enjoying being wet."

With that said the cocoonmum opened her bag and took out her ceremonial instruments to cut open the cocoon. She coached Bev as she went, "Okay, Bev, I'm going to begin. It's very important that you hold very still and do not push or move. I'm going to make my first cut now."

The cocoonmum took a pointed knife and cut a small hole in the bottom of the cocoon where Bev's head was. Then she took a scissors and put the blunt end into that cut and lengthened the opening. Bev's face was the first thing visible as she gasped for a breath of fresh air. The cocoonmum took a cocoon fabric towel and dried her face. Then she continued with the careful task of cutting away the cocoon. She gave the fabric great attention to preserve it for the use in garments that Bev could wear her whole life and her descendants too.

When the cocoonmum got to the waist she put the scissors deep inside the cocoon. Then she cut away the waist strings that went all the way around the entire inside circumference of the cocoon and were attached to Bev's waist.

The cocoonmum commented, "These strings are very strong and fibrous, making them very difficult to cut, but this also makes them extremely useful for the ties of our garments." Then she put the scissors down and dried off more of the moisture that was inside the cocoon. She told Bev, "This water, if we let it evaporate, will carry away with it your body's heat and you will get cold, which would not be good. We're about half done now and soon you will be finished."

As the cocoomum continued, she cut the top half of the cocoon away, which was over Bev's lower body. Soon her painstaking work got her to the end of the cocoon. This part, like the midsection, had special attachments to hold the butterfly securely to the cocoon and to the branch it was spun on. The cocoonmum switched scissors and used a much smaller one for this task, which was among the most difficult parts of the process.

She finally was done and she took hold of Bev with both her arms. Holding her firmly, she pulled her out of the cocoon. She dried her again, now completely from head to toe. The cocoonmum placed on Bev the robe which had been prepared for this one special day. She did so with great ceremony and pageantry, tying it on with the special straps saved from another cocoon's waist attachments. She looked at Bev one last time to be sure the garment was on properly and squarely centered. Seeing that it was fine, she gave Bev a nod and together they turned toward Bev's family and friends who had now gathered in mass.

She said in a loud and grand voice, "May I proudly present to you Beverly Branchwhalker!" With that, many butterflies let loose a sigh of relief and they all clapped their hands in a show of congratulations.

Life returned to normal after Bev's cocoon birth. Dewey worked for his father harvesting leaves, stacking them and toting them to the family's cocoon storage barn. He was constantly criticized by his father for not working fast enough, hard enough or long enough. Dewey felt it was unfair that he, as a caterpillar with very short legs, had to try to keep up with his father, whose legs were longer. But Dewey had learned from experience that he was not going to be able to get a word in edgewise when his father was talking.

ED'S COCOON

One morning Marshall, instead of sending Dewey to work on the early harvest, sent him with his brother Ed. Ed led Dewey to the branch he had picked to weave his cocoon on. Dewey sat attentively as his brother quickly spun his cocoon. Ed worked with great haste, unlike what Dewey had been taught in cocoon class and witnessed with his sister, Bev. Ed completed the task in what Dewey felt was record timing. Then Dewey sat in waiting for hours to ensure his brother would get prompt help from a cocoonmum when he woke, just as his parents had instructed him to do.

When evening came Dewey grew tired but no relief help was sent. Soon the sun set and clouds moved in. The rising moon was not visible for long when clouds and lightening in the distance, began moving in closer. Dewey sat watching and listening, but before long rain started to fall, drenching everything. Still, Dewey sat watching and listening for his brother's cry for help. Dewey was hoping earnestly that something would happen so he could go home. After a while one of his younger brothers came. He said their dad told him, because of the rain, Dewey could come home. So Dewey and his younger brother went home, dried off and went to bed.

In the morning Dewey awoke and rushed out to his brother Ed's cocoon. Because many leaves had come off the tree during the night from the storm nothing looked the same. Dewey found he had to search the branch until he found the cocoon again. Then he sat and waited. About noon the cocoon started to wiggle and move, but Dewey heard nothing. The cocoon continued to move, more and more.

Dewey called out for his brother, "Ed, is that you, are you awake? Ed, why don't you answer me?"

The cocoon started to tear and rip and Dewey became very concerned. This was not the way he was taught or the way he had observed things in the past.

"Ed!" he said, "Something must be wrong with you. I'm going to get a cocoonmum ... don't worry!"

But before Dewey could go any where, the head of a butterfly popped out and said, "Hey, don't go! I'm not Ed."

Dewey was in shock, he stared, and thought to himself, 'This isn't Ed's voice, and this wasn't his face. This isn't Ed.' In a moment, Dewey had composed himself enough to speak, "Who are you?"

The butterfly answered, "Well, I'm McInnus Skyclimber. Who are you and who's Ed?"

Dewey answered, "Ed is my brother and I'm Dewey. My brother was here on this branch in his cocoon last night when I left him. I thought that you were my brother." McInnus struggled to get a shoulder out as Dewey continued to speak, "Can I help you? You shouldn't be doing this alone you know! You could get hurt or worse! And you're ruining your cocoon. I'll go and get a cocoonmum. No, wait there is no time. I should help you get out myself maybe."

McInnus answered, "NO! What are you talking about, help me? You can't. I've got to do this on my own! What kind of caterpillar are you anyway?"

Dewey, still in a panic said, "Well, I just wanted to help, but if you insist, then OKAY"

Dewey sat watching McInnus struggle tediously for several hours to get free of his cocoon. Finally, exhausted, McInnus was completely out and he climbed into an upright position on a smaller branch and held on firmly. His wings were soaking wet and heavy with water. McInnus adjusted his position to allow his wings to hang freely downward and open fully. The weight of the water pulled them from a fan folded position to a fully extended form, like a leaf bud unfolding extremely fast. The water slowly dripped off and evaporated in the warmth of the sun's rays. Soon the wings were completely dry and as the sun shone through their transparent surface, a rainbow formed on the other side.

McInnus, who was now looking and sounding refreshed, looked to Dewey and thanked him for not helping. Then as he flew away he said, "I'll come back to visit you another day Dewey."

Dewey watched McInnus fly away and disappear into the distance. Then he realized he had totally forgotten about his brother Ed. "Oh my gosh!" he said out loud, "I had better find Ed."

So he scampered up the branch in search of his brother's cocoon, but he did not find it. He came back down the branch, retracing his steps. He carefully looked harder than ever to spot his brother's cocoon, but still no sign of it. He worried the cocoon might have been damaged in the storm and knocked off the tree. He continued to look and then on the same branch, very close to McInnus' cocoon, hidden behind a cluster of leaves he spotted Ed's cocoon.

Dewey ran over to it and called out loudly, in joy, "Ed! Ed!" But there was no answer. Dewey ran around to the other side of the cocoon and to his horror it was torn open! "Oh no! What has happened?" Dewey screamed, "I can't believe it, what went wrong?"

Dewey started to cry and ran all the way home to report to his family what he saw. His parents were very disturbed with the report Dewey gave them and they sent for a cocoonmum immediately. When she arrived, they all went out to the branch where Ed had made his cocoon. They saw the two cocoons and the cocoonmum inspected them both very thoroughly. Shaking her head, she said, "What a waste, a total waste of cocoon fabric."

Dewey watched her as she stood by the cocoon McInnus had woven. Then she spoke out, "I can tell by looking at Ed's cocoon here next to me that the storm has severely damaged it. It could even have been a lightning strike. At any rate, Ed did not survive the storm and his body has, unfortunately, been lost as well."

Dewey's mother cried out in tears, sobbing and moaning all the way home. The family stayed indoors the rest of the day and the cocoonmum remained and attempted to comfort the family.

The cocoonmum offered to put Dewey to bed, due to the lateness of the hour. She used that time to caution Dewey privately. She told him that the flying species of butterfly who had made his cocoon on their tree had no business being there and that it was unfortunate Dewey had to be a witness to their barbaric cocoon birthing process. She explained that it would be better if he just forgot the whole thing and told no one else about it either. Especially since he needed to mourn his brother's death and get over that.

After tucking him in and wishing him a good night's sleep, she went out to speak with Marshall and his wife. Among other precautions she said, "It would have been better if Ed, as well as Dewey, had been more closely watched. Now you must watch Dewey especially well, with all that he has been witness to and experienced today."

DEWEY SPINS A COCOON

Summer was nearing as it always did, that the butterflies could be sure of. Dewey wished to himself that things were different. He really wasn't looking forward to the next several weeks. This would be the time that he would have to prepare for leaving his caterpillar adolescent life behind and become an adult, a butterfly.

It spite of all the things he had learned, done and prepared for he felt very unprepared. 'Worse even,' he thought to himself, 'than if I had done nothing or received no help at all.' Things did not feel right to him, but he did not know why or what else they could be like if they weren't this way. The more he dwelt on it, the more he felt confused. He could not put a name on his feelings and that made him feel even more down.

Dewey could tell his time to spin his cocoon was just about here. So he went to his mother and shared this with her, hoping that she would reach over and hug him. Or even better, brush his antenna for him as she had after his fall from the tree in his early days. But instead, she silently nodded her head and said that they would be watching and would be ready when the time came.

Dewey disappeared into the branches of the tree and then walked down to the ground below to be alone. He saw a puddle of water and slowly walked over to it to get a drink. As he bent his neck down to reach the water he saw his reflection and thought to himself that this would be the last time he would see himself in this form. Soon he would change into an adult butterfly. As his mouth touched the water it sent small waves rippling across the surface and erased his image. He walked away and sat down to think.

He was not looking forward to this event in his life. It was not feeling at all like what he had been taught to expect. He was confused and tried to ponder the things he had seen recently. His sister's cocooning, and his brother's disappearance and seeing McInnus coming out of his cocoon. He knew what he was taught and that to do otherwise was not safe because he could lose the support he knew he needed to get started in life living on their tree.

Dewey wandered back home and on the way he looked for a branch where he could spin his cocoon. He was not feeling very energetic and all the branches he looked at seemed the same to him. He could not understand what made a butterfly pick one branch over another. None of them looked very much like something to get all excited about. Anyway, he knew he needed to pick one and since he could not see that one might be better than another, he simply closed his eyes, spun around and pointed randomly. When he opened his eyes he saw the one that he was pointing to and said "That's the one, for better or worse."

The next morning he woke up early. But, instead of getting up, he rolled over in bed and tried to get back to sleep. But sleep didn't come to him. So he laid in bed for a very long while thinking about whatever came to his mind. His thoughts wandered carelessly, but not without the same continuing uneasiness that he felt the day before. Dewey could not make sense of it all, but he knew that he must do what he was taught. Eventually he did get up and start to move about.

His mother asked him, "Are you feeling OKAY? This is not like you to be staying in bed so late in the morning?"

Dewey explained he was just taking his time this morning and did not want to deal with feeling rushed. He hoped his mother was not in a talkative mood because he was feeling like shutting off the outside world.

Dewey hastily finished his morning routines and went outside. He felt like running away but had no idea where he would go. He slowly walked to the branch he had ended up picking the day before and prepared himself for the spinning of his cocoon.

He began by hanging upside down and spinning his hind feet and tail to the tree. Then he continued to spin and weave his lower body into the cocoon. He could not shake that feeling, the one he could not find a word for. He made his waist straps and reinforced the cocoon's hold on him with them. Then he went to work with weaving his upper half. He tried not to let those memories and feelings influence his concentration.

Soon he realized it was not the cocoon spinning he was doing that made him feel this way. Actually, he found that he really enjoyed this task. As he continued he found he was less preoccupied with feeling down. In fact, he was feeling a sort of inner excitement and fulfillment by spinning his cocoon. He wished that his spirits had been this high when he started, but was glad for it now.

Soon he was making his final touches on the cocoon and was feeling secure in the snugness it offered. He could hear his family's familiar chatter in the background and thought to himself that he had selected a place farther away from home than that. It did not matter now though, he was falling fast asleep.

Dewey's family sat vigil to watch his cocoon very closely in hopes that all would go well. They had already lost one son and because of his mother's insecurity with life after she was bitten by one of the mocking birds, the family and the cocoonmum both felt that she simply could not deal with losing another son. Especially not Dewey, who could have died when he walked off the tree, or as his mother remembered it, almost did die when he fell off the tree. Anyway, they all took turns, in pairs, closely watching, listening, and hoping that all would go well.

As the wind picked up they saw some movement and heard some rustling sounds in the cocoon. So they didn't even wait for Dewey to call out for help. They sent, not one, but two of the young caterpillars to get the cocoonmum. They waited with anxious and impatient fear. The cocoonmum could not arrive soon enough to please them and so they sent another pair of their young caterpillars to see what was taking them so long.

Well, very little time had actually passed and the cocoonmum did arrive. You could see by the look on her face that she too was in a hurry. She hadn't even gotten to the cocoon and she already had her ceremonial cocooning instruments out of her bag and was ready to cut. As she approached the cocoon she asked the mother if she was sure this is the right cocoon! The mother screamed, "Yes! What are you waiting for? Cut already!"

The cocoonmum hastily called out to Dewey, who was not really awake yet. He did say 'yes' to her, or so she said. But in his half awake, half asleep state he would have said anything to anybody talking to him and not have been able to remember it.

So the cocoonmum started her first cut and cautioned Dewey to stay very still. Her voice shook with nervous energy and if Dewey had been more awake, he would have been nervous to see how quickly the cocoon birth was happening. It really seemed like the cocoonmum was more interested in preserving the cocoon and pleasing Dewey's parents than helping Dewey to a meaningful cocoon birth.

Even though Dewey was hardly awake, she started asking him questions. His answers didn't seem to match very well, but she continued on giving him instructions as she went. It seemed as though the cocoonmum was cutting quicker than she had ever done before and she was watching Dewey's parents more than the cocoon she was cutting into. The birth happened so fast that at the end, Dewey was still very drowsy and the cocoonmum looked worried.

As she pulled Dewey out from the cocoon, he was not smiling as do most. A butterfly should be able to stand at this point and he wasn't. He wasn't even moving. So the cocoonmum set him down. She laid him on his stomach and pounded him on his back several times. Then she grabbed his elbows and pulled them up toward his head. Placing her hands on his back again she pushed down hard and slowly repeated these steps over several times. Finally Dewey began to cough and gasp for air. She walked around to his feet and slapped them several times.

After this, she returned to the ritual drying off of the new butterfly and the presentation. She placed the robe on Dewey that his family had prepared for him and tied it securely. Then she turned to him and whispered into his ear that he was done with the birthing process, to which he said, "Huh, what?"

Disregarding his comment entirely, the cocoonmum said to the crowd loudly, "May I proudly present to you Mister Dewey Branchwhalker!" Then she sat down for a rest, looking exhausted.

Dewey's family ran over to him and all hugged him, giving him congratulations without end. Dewey was just now slowly figuring out what had happened. Realizing he had more or less missed his own cocoon birth and that his back and feet hurt, he felt anger and regret. It felt like he was robbed and yet he knew he could not criticize his parents or the cocoonmum for doing their duties. So, instead, he went along with the crowd.

He wanted to enjoy what was left of his cocoon birthday, so he played along with it like it was all just fine. He preferred to remember it the way it should have happen, the way he was taught in cocoon class and learned from having seen other cocoon births. He acted as though it was all just fine. He went to his party and after a while he found he was so convincing that even he was able to believe that everything had gone fine. As a matter of fact, he enjoyed remembering it that way better, this way his anger and regret submerged.

BUTTERFLY RENAISSANCE
CHAPTER FOUR
MOVING UP AND OUT

As was the right of every butterfly in the society, or so they all were taught to believe, Dewey could pick his own branch to live and flourish on. The lower branches were well populated and there was not much of value available to choose from, unless of course you had something to offer of substance in exchange for the branch. What wasn't already taken on the lower parts of the tree was not of much value. Those branches tended to be old and not much for producing many leaves for the space they took up. They were also supporting many other branches and had a lot of traffic on them.

Dewey was not one to throw his inheritance away on something he could develop on his own, so his choice was something of a surprise to his family when he announced that he was going to homestead a branch at the upper regions of the tree. He felt that he needed to consider his long term success and potential over short term goals like a showy, expensive branch that had little growth to offer. Younger and newer branches at the top of the tree had very little in their way to hinder growth and expansion.

His father cautioned him about the practical aspects of this choice, saying he needed to consider the low productivity of the younger, smaller branches, as well as their closer proximity to the sun, which would tend to produce smaller and dryer leaves for the harvest. These leaves would also be stronger in flavor. In addition, this choice would also leave him open to drying out, not to mention the increased risk of being attacked by the Mocking Birds, who would find his branch and house easy prey, being in a less populated area, which was easier for the Mocking Birds to swoop down on. Dewey's father wondered if he really thought this thing through or if he was just trying to take the easy way out. He spoke out, "You must reconsider. You need my help to move and I'm not sure I will give it to you unless you have made a sound decision that I like and agree with."

None the less Dewey had an answer for every objection and concern voiced, just as he was taught in Cocoon Class. "Look at it this way," Dewey said, "if you don't help me move, I will be living at home an awfully long time."

His father did comment that at least he was well taught in all respects, but that he fully expected Dewey's branch to do poorly for quite a few years and that he himself would end up providing for his son's needs, just as he had to provide for one of his older brother's needs too, even though he was considered a mature adult living out on his own now. "OK, Dewey I will help you move, but remember this, the higher you go, the farther you can fall."

With that, Dewey made preparations to move. He packed up his personal possessions, his cocoon clothes, his bedding and his portion of the family food stores. The materials he had for his cocoon house went with him too, much of this was given to him by his family as a gift on his cocoon birthday. These items included many yards of cocoon fabric from many generation for the roof and walls of his cocoon house and storage barns as well as the fresh green twigs he would use for the frame of the buildings. The big day came in the early summer. He and his family, along with a few friends, made trip after trip carrying all of Dewey's belongings up the tall central branch of their tree, which would soon be popping out with new flower blossoms.

When it was all done his mother and sisters spread out lunch for everyone to feast on. Dewey's father, Marshall, said that if he had known in advance that it would have been so much work to move Dewey so far, he would have objected stronger when he had the chance and that he would never forget this as long as he lives. None the less, everyone was glad it was over and ate the leaves and drank the tea like there was no tomorrow.

TO BUILD A COCOON

Most everyone left after lunch but some of the men stayed on for the remainder of the day to help build Dewey's cocoon house and barn. Dewey had plans for a small house, about half the size of what he actually had materials for. No one could understand why he had so much material, enough for a large house, but insisted on a small one. After a short argument with his father, who tried to insist on a big house, they all decided that they had wasted enough time trying to make Dewey see things their way, and that if they didn't start construction soon, they would only have time to build a small one anyway.

The largest green twigs went up first for the main frame. They were tied together with rope woven with cocoon fibers, the central veins of leaves and strands of tree bark. Tree sap was painted on to seal the ropes and protect them from moisture that would lead to rot. Sap was also applied to that twigs to keep them from drying out and getting wet from the rain. A large central arch was first to be completed. Then on it were attached smaller twigs at right angles. Again, these were tied together and painted with sap. Everything was in turn secured to the large branch it rested on by more rope. Last, but most importantly, the cocoon fabric was laid on the frame and secured on it with more rope again.

This was a real experience for everyone because it was such a strong symbol of their society's values and heritage. It was considered a part of Dewey's becoming an adult in the most real and practical way. When the finishing touches were done on the house and the crowd of butterflies had walked through and inspected it thoroughly, they all went outside and opened a vat of nectar and toasted Dewey, his new house, barn and homestead. The men were tired and the sun was making its way down into the horizon and so they all wished him luck, welcomed him to stop by their houses for a visit after he got settled in and then left. Dewey thanked them all for their hard work and said he would look forward to seeing them all after a while.

Dewey thought to himself that even though he had to consider the risks and benefits of his choice and the distance he would be putting between himself and his critics, it would be well worth any suffering he might have to endure. At any rate, he was here and he had to make a go of it now. He had left himself no other choice.

A lot of people who knew Dewey from his birth on were never impressed with him. They felt they saw a pattern of laziness and stupidity. They spoke among themselves about it from time to time and all agreed upon this. Perhaps some of this was true too. Since from the day he was born Dewey did things no other butterfly would do, like walking fearlessly off a tree branch and falling to the ground. Many people thought he probably got brain damage from the accident, while others believed he was just stupid and lazy from birth. In cocoon class he always had questions galore and had used up class time pursuing the answers. When it came time for him to start his own branch and build his own house he not only picked a branch far away from everyone else but made his house much smaller than it needed to be. The entire society knew him as someone who was very different and this did not go over very well. Now that he was out on his own, his father made it no secret that he worried he would have to support Dewey until his young branch became productive. Everyone felt this was clearly his way of continuing to be lazy and get away with it.

Dewey was truly challenged to have a good crop in his first year and he knew this well. But the last thing he wanted to do was go to his father and ask for help because of a small harvest. As he thought about it he came to a new realization, he felt that a lot of this was out of his hands. There needed to be a good amount of rainfall early in the growing year and then a lot of warm sunshine with lighter rains to keep the tree well watered. If there was a bad storm, one with hail or lightening strikes on the tree, it would reduce the harvest. He wondered why no one ever explained this to him in cocoon class and as he thought about it he realized that no one really believed it happened this way. Everyone spoke and acted as though these issues were something they were responsible for. They all worried so about it and yet the truth of the matter was that they really had no control over it. Dewey thought on, wondering what he could control. What were the things that he really could do something about?

Soon the newly opening buds of the tree would be bursting forth with the new leaves of spring and along with them the beautiful flowering blossoms of the crab tree would come out in all their splendor. The freshness of the season's rain and thunderstorms would be enhanced by the sweet smelling nectar of the flowers and that would be like heaven Dewey thought to himself. He wanted to conserve his food stores as long as he could yet, in truth, he didn't really want to eat the food that had been in storage for so long because it was dry and even if he added some water it didn't help much, the taste was also rather bland and unexciting.

Dewey wanted to eat something new and fresh like his new home. He waited to eat the buds of the leaves and flowers until they were at least grown into tender shoots, then he went out to gather a few of the early seasons growth. He could not remember anyone actually gathering at this early time in the season. You see, the butterflies of his society had such a fear of not having enough food that they had built up their food stores well beyond their needs for the next several years. No one else ever had, but he felt it would be OKAY as long as he owned the place and didn't gather too much.

As he looked at the young tender leaf and flower buds he had gathered, he stopped his work to ponder what he was doing. The buds, all folded up tightly and compact would someday soon unfold, push themselves out of the small bundle that they were and become something looking entirely different. As a matter of fact, he thought to himself, so could the seeds he had gathered for food if he let them. And the acorn nuts he cracked open and used for drinking cups could also, by their own accord, crack open in the ground and grow up into a large tree. He was amazed at the way things could and did change, from one state of beauty to another even more beautiful.

Any way his work developing something good to eat was well worth it, because he did discover a few new things. The leaves he had gathered were rather strong tasting, which made them a little unpleasant to eat. But as he thought about his option of eating his food stores, which were dry and tasteless, he decided to mix the two together and wow, what a wonderful combination. The two seemed to balance each other's bad sides out and even better was the fact that he needed only a few of the strong flavored new leaves to add taste to the old leaves.

His discoveries didn't stop there either. As he made tea to drink with his meal, he found it also was way too strong. But if he watered down this concentrate, it was a very fine tea indeed. And as long as he had this new wave of creativity going he decided to blend the new tea with the older tea from his food stores. This was another wonderful discovery of taste like he had never experienced. This was one meal he really did enjoy.

He made a sweet snack from the blossoms he had gathered for his dessert. This too had a strong and different flavor to it, but again Dewey watered it down and experimented with different combinations of nectar from the food stores as well as combining it with teas made from the leaves. He could not believe the success of the day and how his efforts paid off. He would give it more thought tomorrow.

In the morning Dewey got up and went outside to stretch and get himself some breakfast. But before he could get to the cocoon storage barn he saw something he didn't like, a flock of hovering mocking birds. They came down from the sky like a raging storm, about two dozen of them in mass. They flew over and then circled back down and around to the branches in formation. As they landed Dewey could feel the branch bending under the added stress of their weight. The larger ones, like bullies came directly to the house, calling out with their hideous screams. The others went to the cocoon barn and tried to get the food stores. The largest ones at the house came with a look of determination and no fear. They would turn their heads sideways and look closely in the windows, and then poke holes in the roof and walls squawking all the while. They seemed to be trying to remove the cocoon covering the frame of sticks but made very little progress because it was very securely in place. This seemed only to infuriate them more.

One stuck his head in the door but the frame was too small for him to enter, although he did try to break it and squeeze in any way. He spread his huge wings out and they covered the house. Then he flapped them and the wind from them shrilled through the windows and left Dewey with a very cold sweat. The angered bird cawed with monstrous screams. His disgusting breath smelled of rotten worms and as he shook with madness he left dust and feathers which smelled of garbage. He just stood there and screamed, extending his neck in an attempt to reach Dewey any way he could. He would snap his beak in the air, as if to warn him by a demonstration of his intentions.

The whole time Dewey's branch bobbed up and down, and back and forth as in the worst of storms. What did they care if it bent to the point of breaking and Dewey fell, crashing to the ground to his death. They would just fly away.

After the attack Dewey went outside to view the damage done to his house and cocoon storage barn. To his surprise it was very light, his house had only a few small tears in it which he could mend and only two holes in it, which he could patch. He had left the large doors to his cocoon storage barn open and the birds were able to fit inside these, there was some food missing but the cocoon storage barn itself was completely intact. He looked inside his vats of nectar and the mocking birds had left them untouched. But seeing the seal broken on one of them he looked in side, it smelled funny and so he got a cup and took a small sip. It had turned rotten, he spit it out saying, "A butterfly could get sick from drinking this wretched stuff." Looking inside his water vats he saw that they too were left alone.

He saw his reflection in the surface of one of them and he thought to himself, 'So this is what I look like now, not very impressive, no wonder the birds attack flightless butterflies.'

Dewey was unhappy with being attacked. This time it was much different than before. Here, it was his house, his branch, his food and his life. He felt more threatened than ever before. His father was not here to watch over him, to assure him after the attack that things would be OK, that the damage to the house and barn could be repaired.

Dewey sat and thought to himself for the remainder of the day. He recalled all of the times the birds had attacked and stolen food or damaged their property. He remembered the time they bit his mom's antenna, and she poked them back in the eye. He would never forget the way the bird was injured. He stopped thinking, and said to himself, 'What if they got poked in the eye again, or worse what if they got poked in the chest, what would happen?'. Dewey decided to do something with that, to somehow build a way to fight back.

BUTTERFLY RENAISSANCE
CHAPTER FIVE
DISCONTENTMENT

Dewey had worked hard to be a success and in his own eyes he was at times very much a success. Even still he longed for the approval and acknowledgment from others, mostly from his parents or at least one family member but he felt as though he got none. He knew that this drove him to work harder and become more productive filling his storage barns but he himself still felt empty inside. He knew that he had been one of the best students in cocoon class, but the one who was best got all the recognition, he got none. Being second best was a disappointment to him. No matter how close he came to being in first place it was never good enough for him or others.

He tried to encourage himself, as long as no one else was going to. After all what harm could it do? He thought about his successes so far and listed them in his mind. There was not dying when he was so young and walked off the tree and also doing so well in cocoon class. There was the fine cocoon he spun for himself and the strong garment it now made. The branch he selected had so much potential for growth and good harvests, with an unending supply of new branches coming off it every year since no one lived above him to lay claim to the tree's growth.

But as he rehearsed in his mind what he felt were positive moments and accomplishments, he could also hear his other thoughts repeating back to him as had happened so much more often before, these were the negative side of the same things. Why did he feel so down and what could he do for himself to make it change he wondered?

Dewey tried to collect his thoughts as he had so many times before in his youth, but they did not come to him. All he could do was think about his cocoon class training and what he was taught.

CONVERSATION WITH HIS FATHER

Dewey had not been living out on his own that long, but perhaps the loneliness of being high in the tree was playing a role in his feeling down, he thought. So he decided to go to visit his father and spend some time with him. When Dewey arrived at his father's branch, he found him hard at work, picking leaves that he would stack and then carry to his storage barn. Dewey said, "Hi Dad, how are things going?"

His father responded saying he was "... very busy, I'm right in the middle of a big harvesting project and why aren't you doing the same?"

Dewey was disappointed that his father did not give him a warmer greeting, but returned an answer saying, "Well I wanted to visit and talk with you. I've been away for a while and I thought I should stop by and let you know how I'm doing."

All the while his father kept picking leaves and stacking them neatly, "Oh, yeah, well, okay, ah, what ever, so talk."

Dewey spoke out saying, "Well, I've been alone for a while and I was worried that...,"

His father impatiently interrupted, "Come on, I don't have all day."

Dewey felt hurt and angered this father had interrupted him as he searched for something to say. Why couldn't his father just stop working long enough to say 'Hi' a little more like he meant it? "I was worried that maybe I would forget how to talk without someone to talk with. Anyway, my friend McInnus hasn't visited me for a while and I'm not sure he knows where I live. So if he comes around here to visit, would you give him directions to my new home for me?"

His father, broke away from his work for a second and then started up again, "You mean that flying butterfly you met the day we lost your brother Ed?"

Dewey said "Yeah, him."

His father spoke out, "I don't see what you could gain by having him for a friend. You two have nothing in common."

Dewey felt defensive and maybe that he had said the wrong thing, so he opened his mouth to defend his friendship and the common things they did share,

"Well, his life is a lot different than mine but, I do like him because he does fly. I saw him with my own eyes and I was impressed with his hard work ethic, it's sort of like ours. The way he broke out of his cocoon proved that, especially after I offered him help and he refused it."

His father stopped his work entirely and turned to face Dewey, "Listen son, I don't think you should have anything to do with him and his kind. I know what they do to their cocoons, what a waste. I don't believe you should work hard to weave and spin a fine cocoon and then destroy it by breaking out of it, what a waste. Its fabric is ruined. I don't call that a work ethic, I call it destructive."

Dewey felt his father had missed his point and was being rather hard on a butterfly he had never met, "Yeah, but I've been thinking and I just realized that the only two real differences between us and them is that we don't break out of our cocoons, they do and we don't fly but they do."

Dewey's father was not happy with his son talking like that, not at all, "What a waste, what a waste! They have to fly to get to warm weather because they don't have cocoon houses to hibernate in and cocoon storage barns to store food in for the winter! They don't store food because they don't have anything to store it in! There are a lot of big differences!"

Dewey felt he had to say something and defend what good points he had made, even though his father was making sense too. "Well, I don't think that the flying butterflies are bad butterflies. Why, I could even enjoy their lifestyle equally well. Sometimes I have even secretly wished I could have been born a flying butterfly and flown when I fell off the tree as a young caterpillar instead of crashing and ending up with a name like Dewey!"

Dewey's father broke in before Dewey could go on, "Dewey! You don't know what you're saying. For one thing, if you were going to be the kind of butterfly who does fly, it would have happened by now. Some butterflies don't fly, I don't know why, I just know they don't and that's the way it is. The sky is blue, the leaves and grass are green and you're not the kind who flies. Like me, like your grandfather and just like your great grandfather, for three or four generations. Like begets like. You don't fly and neither will your children fly. That's the way it was for me and that's the way it will be for you, count on it. When you need help in life it's going to come from your own kind, so it's better not to have friends like McInnus, or harbor secret 'wishes' like wanting to fly, because you only set yourself up failure in our way of life by doing that."

This reaction by his father surprised him, a lot. Then he thought and was surprised at the words that had just come out of his own mouth. He had only just begun to realize what he had said under pressure from his father, in defense of his friend McInnus and how strange it was to now consider it. He had not really ever admitted to himself these feelings and thoughts. They had up until now only been at the edge of his mind. He felt insecure and worried that he had offended his father, so he spoke hoping to mend the division, "You're right, I know exactly what you mean. You're right and it has affected my thinking. I mean, just listen to how I've been talking, like I forgot everything I was taught in cocoon class and I finished second to the top."

His father returned to his work, "That's right Dewey, now you're back on track, just keep that up and you will be fine. Swing by again when you're in a better mood, but right now I've got to get back to my work."

VISITS THE COCOONMUM

Dewey felt a struggle, it reminded him of when he was spinning his cocoon. He went home and rested. The conversation with his father had tired him not just physically but also emotionally as well. He was shocked at the independence he took in talking with his father, saying things that he really hadn't even been willing to admit to himself before. Now he had no choice but to face these issues and live down the fact that now at least one other person besides himself knew also. Dewey thought he should get up and eat supper, but he wanted to rest just a little while longer. He slowly drifted off to sleep and woke in the morning feeling more at ease and rested. He got out of bed and went about his chores with a certain excitement, eating on the run and hoping for something extra to come along and brighten his day. He produced a great deal of work, stacking leaf after leaf and making large neat stacks with them. Then he carried his work to the cocoon storage barn, moving it to the back and rotating his older inventory forward.

Lunch came and went and he was back on the branch doing his work, selecting ripe leaves that were fully grown and full flavored, picking, stacking and toting them to the cocoon storage barn. The sun began to set and Dewey realized he needed to start back to his cocoon house because it was getting too dark to see the way.

Back inside his little house he dished up his dinner and sat to ponder the day. He remembered how he had hoped for something out of the ordinary to come his way but it didn't. This made him wonder how often in an adult butterfly's life do you get to do something other than work sun up to sun down. From what he could remember of his life growing up, that was about it for his fathers life. Also, if cocoon class was any reflection of what to expect, and of course it was, he didn't have much to look forward to. There were to be expected, visits from friends or neighbors, the festivals in the mid summer and fall. But his visit with his father was more troubling than he cared for and Dewey didn't think much of the festivals, just a lot of butterflies trying to show off in front of each other. Dewey felt he was missing something but what it was, he had no idea.

The cocoonmum had counseled him and his family in times of trouble in the past and now he had, perhaps a good reason to see her again. He knew that if he needed help, any of the cocoonmums were helpful people and would fill him in on anything he might have missed. So in the morning he journeyed down his branch to seek out a cocoonmum to speak to. He arrived in no time at Cocoonmum Hasselmeyer's house and knocked at the door.

She greeted him with a great big "Hello, and what may I do for you? Have you come to me for help in selecting a wife? No, no that's not it, I can tell. Let me guess again, you have a dispute over harvesting rights on your branch with your neighbors? Ah, no, that's not it either is it. OKAY, I've got it, you have an injury and you need medical help. That's it, what did you injure?"

Dewey was a bit surprised by her greeting. He had hoped to have spoken earlier but had no chance. Now he did not know what to say because she thought she could guess and get it right. He did not want to disappoint her, nor did he want to be dishonest. He spoke out hoping to not anger her. "Hi, ah, I'm Dewey Branchwahlker, and I'm okay. That is, I'm not hurt or anything like that. And, you're right, I don't need a wife right now and there is no dispute between my neighbors and myself over harvesting rights. I don't really have any neighbors you see, because I live way up high on one of the top branches."

The cocoonmum could be seen smiling big and brightening up a lot after Dewey told her that she was right, "Oh, yes, yes I know who you are now. I remember you're the one who moved way up high on one of the top branches. That's right and you don't have any neighbors, I see. So, I was just having some tea, won't you come in and join me."

Dewey followed her inside her very large cocoon house. He was surprised that she didn't have any windows open, to let in the sunlight and fresh air. Her home was cluttered and it smelled like mold. He sat down as she poured and served him some tea. As he sipped on it he almost gagged, but did not want to offend the cocoonmum. He could not believe how stale it tasted, about ten times worse than his oldest tea. He figured she must have acquired a more sophisticated taste for this kind of old stuff being a cocoonmum. Though he could not remember ever drinking tea this old before. He struggled to find a way to lead into what he wanted to say. "Cocoonmum, I ah, I just had lunch, an early one before I arrived so you will have to excuse me if I don't seem very hungry, or I mean thirsty right now. I really just had a few questions that have been bothering me lately and I hoped you might be able to help me with them. I remember how in the past you had helped my family in that way, with the struggles we sometimes faced."

"Oh, my, yes, I know what you mean, struggles. They always bothered me too. That's why I like to help, but go on."

"Well, I find myself somewhat discontented with my life. I graduated second in my cocoon class, I have a nice house and barn. Between my food stores and my first year's harvest, I have enough food for a long time. As a matter of fact my cocoon storage barn is plumb full to capacity and I am a hard worker. I've been doing a lot of thinking, though. I wonder if this is all there is to my life and what do I really have to look forward to. But I don't feel rich or any better off by it. I have so many questions, I don't understand, like the butterfly I saw break out of his cocoon, he doesn't seem any worse off by it. I don't feel like I'm happy, but I don't know what I'm missing. I'm uncertain about my life. This is the way I felt before I spun my cocoon, not how I felt once I was inside it. I wear my cocoon coat like I was taught, to remind me of that great feeling of accomplishment but, I don't feel that way. Cocoonmum, what am I missing that I still feel this way?"

"Dewey I see this problem a lot. No, not a lot but I see it only occasionally in our butterflies. What it all boils down to is this. Like you said, you have something's in your favor: graduation from cocoon class, a house, a barn, food and a wife. No wait, you're not married. You also had an exceptional childhood, between falling off the tree and everything right on through to being the unfortunate witness to the barbaric birth of that flying butterfly. This has only led to confuse you. You worry too much about the significance of that butterfly's birth. You're an adult now, done with school, your questioning period should have ended a long time ago. If your barn is full, you made it too small.

Anyway you say you feel discontented and you feel like you're not happy and you don't know what you're missing. Well, look at me for example, I'm happy, and the reason is that I have a lot of food stored away. I also have a lot of cocoon fabric to enlarge my house as big as I want, look around and see. I also keep very, very busy. I teach, I help caterpillars out of their cocoons and make them butterflies. I'm a very busy person so I don't have time to ponder all these, these ... what did you call them again ... ? Struggles, that's right. So what I have to say is this, you must have too much time on your hands to get into this kind of a mental jigsaw puzzle with yourself. The answer is simple, you need to work a lot harder, keep very busy, produce food, put it in storage, build another barn, and fill it too. You should have out grown this questioning phase of your life a long time ago. Don't be distracted from your work by spending time on these, these ideas and feelings, or whatever it is that bothers you. You need to grow into a production mode. Fill your barns and you will feel better and find happiness."

Dewey was not sure he had gotten through to the cocoonmum what he had wanted to say, but her tea was even worse warm than hot and so he thanked her for her kind advice and promised to follow it. Then he got up, scooted out the door and went outside taking a deep breath of fresh air. Dewey returned home from his visit with the cocoonmum with as much enthusiasm as he could generate. He felt torn inside. He was no more convinced of her views and values now than before. He continued to have his doubts and feeling of uncertainty, but what else did he have to believe.

He felt that if he simply gave it a total effort and didn't hold back anything at all it would fall into place as the cocoonmum said. He did have to admit the cocoonmum was right when she said he'd had some strange events occur in his life, like being witness to a flying species of butterfly breaking out of its cocoon and some confusing ideas about what it meant. If he wanted a feeling of fulfillment and contentment he must work hard to have full food stores and be done with his work early in the season. Not to have too many goals and not think too much because it is a distraction from his work.

With that Dewey got very busy with his plans. He went right to work harvesting and storing every thing he could. He maximized his time by working sun up to sun down and eating on the run. He skipped many social and family functions just to harvest more food.

Soon he found he had no more work to do on his branches and he decided to search for more things to do. He thought, no one has ever laid claim to the grass on the ground, no one lives there to lay claim to its crops. Everyone eats the grass but they do not harvest it for storage and possible future use. So Dewey set out to do just that. He worked extremely hard to carry load after load from the bottom of the tree to the top. Soon he found his storage areas were full to the brim. He sat and rested that evening hoping he would feel his fulfillment, but none came.

The following morning nothing felt better, no happiness, no fulfillment no sense of accomplishment. Dewey felt empty and disappointed, but he decided to build bigger storage areas and harvest more leaves from the grass. This too left him empty and blue inside. He told himself to rest and enjoy, take life easy for a while and soak in the feeling.

Dewey knew of no other recourse in life but to continue on as he always had. He thought long and hard but the truth of things seemed to be this, hard work did not give him fulfillment. Devotion to the societies' values and beliefs did not give him any comfort. He had full barns but he was himself an empty butterfly. Harder work and greater devotion only made him feel even that much more empty. He knew this was no way to live and for him that meant a lot. He had no fulfillment, no joy, no happiness, but at least now he knew this for certain, he knew where he would not find it. He knew now that he must change. Change in order to survive, in order find the fulfillment he not only craved and wanted but must find in order to have a reason to keep going on in life. He sat for a long time, having come to this realization and made up his mind to change. He felt very lonely and vulnerable. His instructors, his family here on the branch, his friends, no one in the entire society could help him, nor would they want to help him if they knew what he was seeking. He reasoned that regardless of his lack of resources he must somehow find this intangible, indescribable, different way of life. He decided to do it.

BUTTERFLY RENAISSANCE
CHAPTER SIX
DEFENSE SYSTEM

Dewey worried so that the mocking birds would return to his house. He feared that they not only could ruin his branch, the house, the barn and all that was in them but they could hurt him as well. He remembered how they hurt his mom and destroyed their family's property. He did not understand why his society, with all of their efforts to prevent a food shortage, had done nothing to try and prevent the mocking birds from picking on the butterflies.

Dewey's mind would not let this rest. Thoughts churned over and over in him, again and again. His mother poked one in the eye and it hurt that mocking bird. He had drunk rotten nectar and it could have made him sick, what would it do to a thieving mocking bird who might drink it? And what if, somehow, a mocking bird had a run in with those thistles growing on the ground below the tree?

Dewey decided to do something very daring, to fight back against the mocking birds. First he went down to the thistle patch with a cocoon sack and a couple of small twigs. He very carefully picked up about two dozen of them with the twigs and put them in the cocoon sack. Then he tied it shut and dragged it with a cocoon rope a safe distance behind him up the tree to his house and soaked the whole thing, sack and all, in fresh nectar. Next he took the vat of spoiled nectar and put it out in the open with a cup to drink from right next to it, hoping that it would look inviting. Then he gathered up short hard wood sticks from the ground below the tree and painstakingly chewed them down to make very pointed ends. These he took and fixed to the underside of his roof, tying them tightly to the supporting frame with cocoon rope so they were not quite visible, but still able to poke a mocking bird in the eye should he try to take a bite out of the cocoon fabric roof. Last of all he took the bag of thistles out of the vat of fresh nectar and with the small twigs set them on a platter as though they were for a meal. These he placed out next to the vat of spoiled nectar and cup he had set out earlier.

"Now." he said to himself, "I sure hope these are going to work!" Then he went about his daily business. There was no telling where or when the mocking birds would strike next, but oddly enough, Dewey actually hoped it would be soon and that it would be his branch that they would come to.

As if fate were in charge, the mocking birds did come that day and perhaps it was the fact that Dewey had invitingly left out nectar, even though spoiled and a batch of tasty looking treats too. As soon as Dewey saw their shadow, he high tailed it to his house and sat as close as he dared to his window to watch. He knew from experience that some of the mocking birds would go for the food stores while others would come to his house and try to destroy it in order to get at him.

At first they all went for the nectar vat and thistles. Just as Dewey had anticipated they started to gobble down the tasty thistles soaked in fresh nectar. Dewey safely watched from his window as they choked and spit. A few were overcome by the thistles and lost their balance, falling to their death on the ground below. Other birds who were not as bad off went for the vat of spoiled nectar and stuck their heads right inside and drank deeply trying to find some relief. Those mocking birds soon realized what had happened in their panic, that they had drank a lot of spoiled nectar. Several of these birds had had enough and tried to fly away, but as they left the tree, they were only able to at best, glide to the ground below, where they hacked and convulsed until they too died. The few remaining mocking birds, who now were extremely angry with the way things were going, stormed over to the house screaming bloody threats. Dewey, not yet fully confident all of his ideas would work, grabbed a sharp pointed stick and sat in the very middle of this house ready to do whatever he might have to, to defend himself. In only a moment those remaining mocking birds in their anger poked and tore away at the roof of Dewey's cocoon house only to find themselves bleeding and blinded. This about did them in. More than one was now completely blinded, so they moved to fly away. Those completely blinded, unable to see for themselves and without direction from their companions, flew into the tree branches and fell to their deaths below. Dewey came cautiously came out of his house wielding his pointed stick and watched as only three of the original flock were seen flying off in utter and complete defeat.

VISIT FROM COURTLYNN

Dewey returned to his house to see what actual damage had occurred and though it was light, he could see he would have to mend a few tears and patch a few holes. There were blood stains on the fabric as well and not having ever encountered this issue before or been taught anything on it in cocoon class, he had no idea what to do there.

Going to his cocoon storage barn he found nothing was damaged or even touched. He gathered up the thistles and carefully set them inside the barns doors and moved the spoiled nectar vat in there too. Looking down to the ground below he saw his victory over the mocking birds and went off to rest peacefully for the night.

Early the next morning as he started his chores he heard a familiar but uninvited voice calling out from over his shoulder. "Dewey, Dewey Branchwahker!"

He turned to look and confirm his dread. It was Courtlynn from his cocoon class. She, to his surprise, was still a caterpillar, "Oh, hi." Dewey said returning her greeting, "What brings you up this way?"

"Well, there had been such a bad storm last night that I came up here to see if you were okay."

Dewey knew of no storm, though he had slept very soundly after his victory, but he also knew Courtlynn and that she did not always make good sense when she spoke. So he decided to keep things simple and go along with her, "Well I slept very soundly but I did look over my property yesterday and found only minimal damage to it."

Courtlynn responded, "What do you mean, the storm was just last night. Why would you have looked at it yesterday?"

Dewey did not want to tell anyone yet, especially Courtlynn, about his defense system, so he simply said, "Oh yeah, I meant today. You know those storms have a way of ..."

Courtlynn interrupted. "It must have been a terrible storm. I saw a lot of dead mocking birds on the ground below, but you seem to have done well and with only minimal property damage."

"Well you see I've built my house very well, not for size but more for strength."

"Good. Dewey I was wondering whatever did you have in mind when you picked those thistles that you carried up here. They can be so dangerous for a butterfly, if you became entangled in one I mean. You would probably have to have a cocoonmum remove it. But then you would have to explain to her what you were doing with it in the first place, what a mess that will become."

Dewey was getting a little irritated with her rambling and insecure with what she saw, he answered, "Would become, not will become, Courtlynn."

"Oh yeah, I get a little mixed up sometimes. Anyway, I just wanted to say that I saw one in the mouth of one of those dead mocking birds at the foot of our tree. I could tell he had died in the storm along with his companions."

"Dewey," she said, "Why did you build two large storage barns when you could not possibly fill one in your first year of farming?"

Dewey, knew that he could not keep this from Courtlynn. Wanting to show off his productivity and put her mouth to rest, he called her over to show her two large, full to the brim, cocoon storage barns. "Come and look for yourself, I have done what no one believed I could accomplish!" With that he opened his large doors and took her on a tour. He was glowing with pride and he showed off his barns and productivity. He hoped this would impress her into being quiet and leaving.

Courtlynn said nothing until the end of the tour and then opened her mouth, "I know how you struggle with life. There is not enough food here to feed your kind of needs, nor could there ever be even if the whole world were employed." Dewey did not answer her back because he was becoming so quickly irritated with her nonsense answers and comments.

"Well, I going to be off now. Oh, I almost forgot to tell you, there is a meeting of the butterflies in the Great

Hollow of the Tree tonight. Maybe I will see you there and you could be the first to say 'Hi' to me. Bye."

Dewey whispered under his breath "Yeah the first and only one ." Then he went back to his chores and worked hard until about noon when he broke for lunch. He then decided to go ahead and get started on his repairs to his cocoon house. He enjoyed knowing that his defense system had worked exactly as he had hoped. But before long the drudgery of the life of a butterfly set in and he began to feel down, especially while having to fix the roof of his house. Why couldn't he have devised a better way to defend his house so the mocking birds would not have been able to damage it?' he wondered.

CONVERSATION WITH THOMAS

About mid afternoon, as Dewey was in the middle of his repairs and growing tired of them, another one of his friends from cocoon class daze showed up. Thomas, the one involved in the pinching incident, called out to Dewey as he approached. "Dewey, I'm glad I caught you at home. I needed to tell..." He stopped for a moment as he saw Dewey in the middle of his repairs, surprised that a newer built home had need of any, and said instead, "What's wrong?"

"Oh, nothing, and everything." Dewey responded, 'I'm in the middle of these repairs and I would rather be out doing something else."

Thomas replied, "I know what you mean, I'd rather be out gather leaves too."

"No, I don't mean farming, I mean doing something else ... something a butterfly around here would not typically do. Do you know what I mean?"

"No, I don't know, what else is there for a butterfly to do, that we would enjoy more than farming our branches?"

Dewey pondered how he might answer, "I mean ah, discovering the world around us. There's more to life than what we've experienced. Just look, we're here on our tree and there's a whole world out there that we know nothing about."

Thomas was thrown by Dewey's notions and didn't have the vaguest idea what he was driving. "Dewey, I'm well educated, as a matter of fact I finished first in our graduation class. But I have no idea what you mean, so explain yourself."

Dewey was not happy knowing that Thomas had finished first in class, especially after he got off after starting a pinching incident that Dewey alone was chastised for. He felt his anger welling up inside and he spoke strongly trying to show off his intellectual superiority, "All of my life I've been told what to do, told what to believe, told what to think."

Thomas grew distracted from Dewey's comments as he looked at the damage to Dewey's house and the blood stains on the roof. "Did you say something?"

"Yes, I just shared with you how I feel."

"How you feel? Oh, um, I wasn't listening, tell me again."

"What I just said was that all of my life I have never thought for myself, chosen what I wanted to believed in, done what I wanted to do."

"What are you saying? I've never heard of anything like it?"

"What I just told you is that I've never questioned my existence, asked myself what I wanted to do with my life once I became an adult. I'm surprised it didn't come up in cocoon classes. You know when they explain what life is supposed to be like for butterflies! I'm tired of that. I don't like it any more, to heck with that. I have questions they haven't let me ask, questions they probably don't even have answers for."

"What then?"

"What do you mean, 'what then?'?"

"I mean, if you have these all important questions, which I haven't even heard yet, what would you do with the answers? If they even exist, what would you do?"

"I think the answers would lead me to a new and different life of true fulfillment! That's what I would do!"

"This all sounds pretty hoaxie to me, did you get hit in the head or something?"

"No way, be serious."

"Well, then have you been getting enough sleep at night? I'm concerned about you."

"No, I don't actually sleep well at night. Sometimes I just lie awake at night and look out my window at the stars. Then I think about my friend McInnus and what he tells me about his life and what it's like. He's a flying species of butterfly and he tells me about the things he does.   Like instead of hibernating in the winter he and droves of others just like him fly south to were he says it stays warm even in the winter.   He shares with me about what it's like to fly high above the ground and how exciting it is to fly and cut through the winds that come along. He never wears a cocoon coat, and his wings are huge. He says all butterflies were met to fly."

"Okay, okay, now I've heard it all, you were hit in the head weren't you!"

"Knock it off, I'm being serious with you about things I can't even talk to most butterflies here on our tree about and you're making jokes, or not even listening!"

"All right then, you want my honest opinion. OKAY, I think based on the way you're talking that you had your oxygen supply cut off too long while you were in your cocoon. You're talking as though you're full of nonsense and I don't even want to hear any more of your crazy, foolish thinking. McInnus is an uncivilized species of a butterfly who goes around naked without a cocoon coat, probably doesn't even own one, showing off his genetically over sized wings. He has no cocoon house and he has to fly to warm weather because he is too unsettled to store food for the winter and rest with hibernation in the cocoon house he doesn't even have. That's what I think, and if you think differently than me and the rest of our species then why don't you try life the way your friend McInnus lives it.   Soon enough you'll see what difficulties come you're way when you're walking to some warm place in the winter because you didn't do things the way you were taught! Anyway Dewey, tell me what are these stains on your roof, I've never seen anything like it before?"

Dewey felt he had the perfect opportunity to show up Thomas with his successful defense system and so he showed off the whole thing to him, explaining in detail how he built it and the victory he experienced just the day before. Thomas quietly listened but at the end shook his head, saying "Dewey take some free advice, you are a flightless butterfly, and this is the most you can hope for in life. You've always been a problem child, you will always be a problem child. You can't get any more out of life than this and with your two full barns you've got it all already. I've got to get going now."

Dewey said, "Hey, wait you forgot to tell me what you came up here for in the first place."

Thomas laughed, "Oh, it was nothing, I'll tell you next time I see you." With that Thomas was off in a flash down the branch.

MEETING AT THE
GREAT HOLLOW OF THE TREE

When Dewey arrived at the meeting, he was disappointed that it was already underway. He had no idea what the meeting was about and it only further complicated matters not to have been there when the meeting started. He moved about going between the small groups that had formed to discuss the issues. Dewey had never been to a meeting prior to this, as they were only open to adults, but he knew from other experiences that all the meetings the adults had were usually somewhat chaotic. At one cell group he found them discussing how crop yields might go down, but food stores would be safer. At another how repairs to property could be affected, that they may increase or others argued they may go down. Another cell group was talking about cleaning up stains and corpses. Then the last group he checked with spoke of how brilliant Thomas was for inventing a defense system that might work against the mocking birds. Seymour Cytlos was arguing that it might not work at all and only anger the mocking birds to more fearless attacks. Hearing this, Dewey stopped immediately in his tracks and in anger he searched the room for Thomas. His thoughts raced, knowing now that Thomas had taken his ideas and shared them with the cocoonmums as though they were his original ideas.

Spotting Thomas he walked directly to him, and called out, "Thomas, I need to talk to you right now!"

Thomas turned with a large smile on his face which fell as he saw who was speaking to him. "Thomas I know what you've done here. You came up to my branch to tell me about this meeting, but decided not to tell me after you saw my defense system so you could steal my idea for your own, didn't you?"

"Dewey, relax, it's no big deal! You've got nothing to be mad about. I've got everything well in hand. Besides, the cocoonmum probably wants to talk to you. Have you talked to her yet? She is probably upset with you, you know?"

Dewey's heart sank as he heard this, the cocoonmum being upset was not good. "Why, what did I do?" Dewey said.

"Well, you developed this defense system and didn't ask permission first. Then you didn't share it with any one, before or after using it. Then you angered the mocking birds with it." Thomas said.

Dewey didn't even think for himself, he just raced off to find Cocoonmum Kreeper who was conducting the meeting. When Dewey reached her he introduced himself to her, but she didn't say much.

So Dewey talked quickly, "Didn't you want to see me?"

"No." she said, "Why should I have, what did you do?"

"Well, I'm actually the inventor of the defense system. I'm sorry I didn't ask permission to build it, or share it with you sooner. I know I angered the mocking birds, but they are always mad anyway."

Hearing this Cocoonmum Kreeper stopped to think for a moment, then her face became angry. "Yes, Dewey, you're right. I should be mad, that is I am mad at you for this. You didn't ask permission, which you should have done. Then you didn't share it with us, which you also should have done. And I'm sure the mocking birds are angry now, which is not good. Thank goodness for Thomas. He shared it with us though, he will get credit for this much. However, you are to blame for the rest of this situation!"

Dewey's heart sank again, he felt so unfairly treated. Thomas tricked him and was taking credit for the defense system and the now cocoonmum was mad at him too. He walked to a corner of the room and waited.

Soon Cocoonmum Kreeper called everyone to order and spoke out, "We have a lot of differing opinions here regarding the defense system. Some of you suggest the system won't work. Some that if it works it will anger the mocking birds and others think it will work but will also create extra work for us. So what I've decided to do is this, I will do an on site inspection. The following butterflies should accompany me tomorrow at sun up: Thomas Limbcreeper, Seymour Cytlos and Dewey Branchwhalker. I will announce my decision on its value at our next meeting. Thank you all for coming, this meeting is dismissed."

ON SITE INSPECTION

Dewey left in a hurry. He ran home and sat rethinking how Thomas had used his anger, his ambition, his pride and his fears to manipulate. Dewey felt used and foolish. These butterflies would be at his branch first thing in the morning to inspect his invention and Thomas would get credit for it too. Life was so unfair. He tried to sleep, but it seemed all he could do was think over and over how things had gone. It was late in the night before he fell off to sleep.

When Dewey awoke the sun was rising but he felt so tired. He wanted to just roll over and go back to sleep and forget the previous night. He hoped it would all just go away and that he could live his life in isolation.

But he rolled out of bed anyway, warmed some tea for himself and sipped it slowly.

Soon he could see someone coming up the branch, they were alone. As they got closer it was clear to him who it was, "Drat, what else could go wrong today. That's Courtlynn, what does she want"? Soon enough she arrived at Dewey's home and greeted him to which he reluctantly returned a cool response.

"Dewey, I know you a little better than you give me credit for. Act out of place and try letting me be your friend. My wayward words could be helpful to you in ways you don't realize. Guests will be arriving soon and though many disregard me ill witted I at least know which direction to point. Thomas knew how to use you for his own scheme, but I will be here for your good."

Dewey looked up and thought to himself, 'I don't have time to figure out what this immature caterpillar is talking about.' His thoughts were broken by the sound of his 'guests' who had just now arrived.

"Dewey, Dewey Branchwahlker!" called out Cocoonmum Kreeper as she and the others arrived.

Dewey turned to greet them and ignored Courtlynn.

"Thomas, why don't you take us on a tour of the defense system and explain how it works as we go?" said the cocoonmum.

Dewey was not specifically asked to go with so he didn't. He sat and secretly hoped that Thomas might make a mistake and get poked with a sharp stick or get a thistle stuck on himself. He watched from a distance, but the others were very careful to keep there distance from the defense system. He wondered though how would that intellectual type, Seymour Cytlos, get anything out of the tour, Dewey laughed as he thought to himself, he's as blind as a bat. Anyway, as they ended their tour Thomas opened a vat of nectar and took a sip. Dewey held back his laughter, because this was the vat of spoiled nectar. Thomas spit it out, spraying it on everyone with him. Dewey got up, walked over to it very quickly and offered Thomas some fresh nectar. Not that he was so much concerned for Thomas, he just didn't want Thomas to get sick at his house. Then Dewey offered fresh cocoon cloth towels to the others to clean up with. The group then joined together to discuss the defense system and Courtlynn stood close by listening in as they all talked.

Thomas very confidently spoke out, "I think I could install this in any cocoon house in just under three days. For that I would want to be paid six days of harvested food."

Seymour Cytlos objected, as he did to just about everything, "Cocoonmum Kreeper, I have seen nothing here to show that this 'defense system' is going to work. I think what we need to do is to take it apart, study it over thoroughly and set it up on an isolated branch somewhere far away from our inhabited branches. Then observe it for a full three season before we draw any conclusions."

Thomas objected to that, "But Cocoonmum, I assure you it will work. I know it will."

Cocoonmum Kreeper spoke out, "Thomas, I have to agree with Seymour. I have not seen anything here that proves to me it works on anything, anything other than butterflies who drink nectar that is not there own. So unless someone else has something to say, I will have to agree with Seymour." The cocoonmum looked at Dewey as though his credibility was on the line for the invention Thomas would be taking credit for.

Dewey thought, 'I've got nothing to loose here that I haven't already lost and I can just rebuild anything they want to remove from this branch. Thomas could loose his claim if I keep my mouth shut and let that Seymour's idea prevail.' Dewey spoke out after his short silence, "You're right. Thomas has not shown you anything that proves this will work."

"Cocoonmum, wait, I have something to say. It does work, for as surely as his grave was his end, I myself spoke to a dead mocking at the foot of our tree who assures me it did work already." Courtlynn blurted out.

The cocoonmum took offense that this uninvited adolescent caterpillar should speak out. She didn't hear so much what she said, just that she said something. "Young child, your place is not among these adults or myself. We're conducting an important meeting and you're simply disrupting us."

The cocoonmum stopped and thought for a moment before she said anything else. She looked at Courtlynn, then surveyed with her eyes Dewey's branch, then very casually looked down. She turned to Thomas and said, "If this defense system did work, I imagine that any mocking birds killed by it would have fallen directly below us, Thomas. Wouldn't they have, Thomas?"

"Oh, why, ah, yes, that's right cocoonmum, they would have. Let's look and see if any are there now."

Everyone got up and headed down the branch to the main stem to the bottom of the tree and over to the area directly under Dewey's house. Just as could be expected there were several dead mocking birds lying on the ground. As the cocoonmum looked at them she was able to see several thistles stuck in the mouths of the birds and another with an eye poked out, as well as other wounds on his body. Thomas, who had up until now been rather brave and proud of his situation, could be seen not far away looking sick from the sight of the dead birds. The group re-gathered at the base of the tree and all agreed, including Seymour, that the defense system was in fact a success and that it should be shared with all butterflies who might like to have it at their houses too.

The cocoonmum said to Dewey "Perhaps you do have something to offer to your society." Then she turned and asked Thomas to make a detailed presentation at the next meeting at the Great Hollow of the Tree.

After that day Dewey and Thomas avoided each other. Thomas also avoided repeating anything he had heard from Dewey, least others think he was part of the same radical thinking that lead Dewey to talk the way he had about their species way of life. Dewey in turn felt alone, not just because his former best friend didn't want anything to do with him any more, but because he couldn't find anyone in his species who might think or feel like him about their existence. He was much too insecure a person to bring it up again. If his former best friend rejected him, how might others treat him? He couldn't handle any more rejection for now. Instead, he spent a lot of time thinking through his questioning of his existence, what he might choose to do with his beliefs, his life, and tried to clarify exactly what it was that was gnawing at him so unceasingly. He looked forward to another visit from his friend McInnus, but saw nothing and grew discouraged. He withdrew from many things in life, trying to make some kind of sense of it all. He wished McInnus was there.

BUTTERFLY RENAISSANCE
CHAPTER SEVEN
TURNING THINGS AROUND

Dewey had aspirations. He hoped only to achieve a few of the many he had dreamed of. They came to him as he pondered and day dreamed about life as he was taught and lived. Many of these he had seen happen, his own home, his successful defense system, his becoming an adult and ones he had not even thought or dreamed of, his new developments in foods and drink.

Of his most lofty aspirations, flying, was one that he had chosen not to give up on. He had a few ideas on how this one might be worked out. Because he was a butterfly of much thought and had the time on his hands, he was able to consider many of the aspects of flying. He knew from experience that his species, which was to his dismay a non flying species, was for all he could tell totally the same as the flying species in every respect in their childhood, size, diet, physical appearance and markings.

But, what gave him the most unanswered questions was why he was cocoon-birthed with the help of a cocoonmum and his friend, McInnus and his species were not. It was after this event that the outward differences in the two species really became apparent. He and his species were dark and un-colorful, while they were beautifully colored and majestic. He was stout and stubby with short, dwarf like wings that really seemed to serve no purpose. He had been taught that butterflies were like the birds, some flew like the eagle and some did not like the chicken and turkey. His friend McInnus and his species came out of their cocoons without help and could fly, yet he could not. Dewey reasoned to himself that this might have something to do with the questions he was seeking answers to.

One enjoyable sunny Saturday afternoon Dewey was contemplating plans for his life. Among the most important of his ambitions in life was to be able to fly. Somehow, some way he wanted to be able to at least experience just once the act of flight. He had given the idea much thought and now had several ideas in mind on how he might be able to achieve this dream of his. His first notion on how to start was to enlist the help of his friend from childhood, McInnis. He was going to be coming over soon, as he did more often lately on weekend to visit and enjoy Dewey's company. As a child Dewey had been told to avoid McInnus by his parents, but in secret he maintained the bonds that were formed between them from the day they met, McInnis' cocoon birthday. Now, as adults they were able to met without the fear of his parents finding out he was being disobedient. If someone saw them together as adults, while it wouldn't go over so well with Dewey's society he at least would not be punished. The flying and non flying species of butterflies did interact on occasion and always on a peaceful level.

Dewey didn't even need to turn around to look, he could tell the shadow appearing over his shoulder and the soft flutter of butterfly wings meant that McInnus was now landing on his branch. He turned to the side and greeted his friend and offered him some fresh nectar. McInnus drank it quickly, being tired and thirsty from his flight to Dewey's house. McInnus offered Dewey some young flower blossoms, which had not yet even fully opened. They would make a nice summer nectar, a strong full flavored one. They talked casually for a while, catching up on each other lives. Dewey spoke about his hopes for a more plentiful harvest so he could store even more food.

McInnus' life was very different. He spoke of his journeys to many different parts of the region, how he found food abundantly available where ever he was. How he worked hard to strengthen himself in preparation for his migration to the South for the winter season. This would be his first and it was very exciting to him. It was all he could think about most days.

Dewey changed the subject after McInnus had finished sharing his excitement. "McInnus," he said, "for a long time now I've been giving some thought to the notion that someday I would like to fly and be like you. My family has told me this will never happen and that I'm not meant to fly. But I've been giving a lot of thought to it, a lot of hard thought as matter of fact." McInnus wasn't at all sure where this was going to lead, but he sat patiently and nodded his head and listened.

Dewey went on "I've got several ideas in my mind. I'm not sure which one of them might work. From what I've been able to learn about flying over the years, which actually isn't much, I have decided to ask you for some help with one idea. What do you think?"

McInnus was silent for just a moment, in surprise and awe at what Dewey was saying, then he spoke. "You know that in my community our beliefs are very different than what you were taught to believe. I've always sought to respect you, your society and its right to choose. I think you might know that I believe every butterfly was meant to be able to fly, everyone. I would love to be of help in any way I can to you so that you can fly."

Dewey was overjoyed. He was so nervous about asking, he knew very little about the other butterflies and what they believed. "Great!" He shouted, "Here's my plan. I was thinking that what would be the easiest would be, if you're willing, to have you climb up on top of me, on my back, grab hold of my wings with your hands and feet and lift us both together into flight."

McInnus agreed and they went to stand on an open part of the branch so they would not have to contend with flying around other smaller branches. Dewey stood by, anxious but not too fearful to go ahead,

McInnus was confident with himself and his flying ability, which was second nature to him. As they stood together, ready for flight, McInnus grabbed hold tightly and started to move his wings, telling Dewey to get ready. He flapped his wings for a while, expecting to go somewhere, but they did not move. So he shook his head, grunted and again flapped his wings vigorously with all his might. But still they did not move. Dewey had not yet figured out that, for some reason, it wasn't going to happen. McInnus let out a small sigh and stopped. Then he moved to return to Dewey's house.

Dewey, not aware of the failure, said "Hey! What's going on? Where are you going?"

McInnus simply said, "I don't understand it, we're not going any where. I tried with all my might and we still didn't move."

Dewey, disappointed and let down, turned and walked back to the house too. McInnus, shaken in his confident flying skills looked to Dewey and said, "I'm sorry I let you down. I don't understand why I could not lift you into flight. I have to go home now."

Dewey, who was already trying thinking of another way to fly, did not see the disappointment on McInnus' face or hear it in his voice, he simply said "Good bye."

SEES HIMSELF IN THE NECTAR VAT

As Dewey went about his daily work he stopped to draw a sip of nectar from a large storage vat sitting just outside his cocoon storage barns' doors. He filled his cup and drank deeply to quench his parched throat. Then turning back to the vat to get a second drink he moved to dip his acorn cap cup and stopped, seeing his shadow in the bottom of the vat. Slowly he let his eyes refocus to the surface of the nectar. Its red tint, shining in the suns' rays, had added an appearance of colors to his dull image. Dewey was stunned to imagine himself as any color other than his brown coat. He looked hard and long, like in a day dream, only to be reawakened to the day by a strong breeze that had come along stirring up the nectar and sending ripples across its surface.

Dewey was determined not to lose sight of his reflection despite the distortion it caused. He concentrated his thoughts and focused hard. To his utter surprise what he was able to see nearly knocked him off his feet. The ripples on the surface of the nectar had magnified his stubby and misshaped wings into large majestic wings, just like his friends, McInnus. He stayed starring in awe and bewilderment until the breeze passed and the ripples of the waves disappeared, taking the appearance of his large wings with it. He thought to himself, 'With wings like that I could fly.' He stood there in silence and waited. He wished the moment could last for ever. Dewey started to come down off his emotional high and he could feel his heart still beating fast, pounding hard and strong. Slowly he relaxed and his heart beat slowed but he committed to memory his moment of glory, even if it was only an illusion.

FEATHER CRAFT

Dewey's imaginative mind had created for him an option beyond his hopes that McInnus could help him fly. After the last attack of the Mocking Birds, Dewey had gathered tail and wing feathers that they lost in the battle and stored them secretly in his house. He used twigs and cocoon straps along with the feathers to fashion a craft with wings that resembled the contour of a flying butterfly's wings. He built a platform under it to ride on. He had to work on it at night for fear someone would see him from a distance and come to see what it was. He stored it in the cocoon barn during the day, covering it with leaves in case someone might wander in there and discover what he was doing.

With a concentrated effort it was ready in just over a week. Dewey had been taught to avoid crashing of any kind and so this was a real trial of his hopes and his education. If he didn't try, he might never fly, if he did try he might crash. But after a few more days of contemplating, he did decide to chance it, because if he could not reach his goals, he had nothing. Dewey worried someone might see him and if they did he would be rejected for building the craft and believing he might fly. Dewey reasoned the best time to try was not at night, when he would not be able to see what was happening. But at the crack of dawn it wasn't likely anyone would be up yet and all he needed was a moment to fly far enough away so he could land the craft out of view from the tree.

Dewey didn't sleep well that night, he dreamt off and on, but could not remember about what as he woke through the night. He wasn't sure how soon the dawn would rise but felt lying in bed was of no use any more. He rose and went to the barn, uncovering his craft and inspecting it one last time. He moved it to the doorway and positioned it toward the horizon. Then he waited anxiously.

Soon things had lightened up enough and he prepared himself for the moment. Moving the craft out to the edge of his branch and holding tightly with his hands, he rested his body on the platform. Then he pushed with his hind legs till the craft teetered forward and back several times. Then he leaned forward and slid off the branch. Before long his arms began to ache from holding so tightly. But with his eyes opened wide and his antenna standing upright he hoped to make it past a small hill just up ahead and land on the other side. That way the craft would be well hidden from his society. He looked forward, but did not see the horizon or the hill. Instead the craft was pointed downward and was spinning round and round. Dewey held even more tightly, he rolled upside down several times as the craft spun sharply toward the ground, picking up speed all the while. He was headed to the bottom of his tree. He felt sick to his stomach and the thought of being caught caused him to panic as his hands, now trembling in weakness, slipped and he flew out of the back. He could see his craft fast approaching the ground and as it crashed it broke up into many pieces, which in turn scattered in the wind.

Then Dewey landed with a hard bump to the ground. He didn't move, he didn't think, he just went blank and waited for a while.

As he came to his senses he was glad he was alive, but he could not stop himself from worrying that someone might see the remains of his feathered craft and him near it. Dewey got up and looked around, seeing no one he gathered his wits and scampered up to his branch and stayed put the rest of the day.

PHYSICAL TRAINING

All summer Dewey continued his plans and worked on his secret ambition, to fly. He trained himself vigorously, going to a distant place away from his tree, where he felt sure no one would ever come. It was barren and somewhat dry there, with a lot of rocks that he would use for lifting like weights. He would run sprinting and going greater and greater distances to increase his endurance. He found that if he hid large rocks inside the pockets of his cocoon coat no one back at his tree would notice and it helped with his muscle development. He was so busy with all of his efforts to become stronger that he had little time to notice the wear and tear on his cocoon coat and mend it as all butterflies had been trained to do in butterfly classes. When the other butterflies saw him they treated him poorly because they viewed anyone who didn't keep up their appearances including their cocoon coats as inferior. As the rocks in his pockets helped him grow stronger they also stretched the garment into a larger size and this helped to hide the increase in his body size. No one noticed how big his muscles were becoming, or how productive he was able to be because of his superior physical conditioning. They just continued to think of him as the strange and weak one that he had once been.

BUTTERFLY RENAISSANCE
CHAPTER EIGHT
THE MID-SUMMER FESTIVAL

It was at the mid-summer festival that Dewey unexpectedly surprised everyone, including himself and in more ways than one. Along with the food and socializing were the summer games of tree climbing and foot racing. Dewey was very tired of being looked down on, something he felt he did not deserve. He felt very confident that he would be able to compete well in both of these events and would be able to surprise everyone by being a top contender not just in the races but also in agricultural events as well with his food and beverage entries.

As Dewey approached the registration booth he could see the butterflies looking his way and talking amongst themselves. He had no idea what they were saying and it made him feel a bit self-conscious. As he got closer one butterfly nudged another one and then they stopped talking suddenly and looked away in silence.

"Hello, what beautiful weather we're having for our festival today." Dewey called out. Not a one of them returned his greeting and he, though feeling even more self-conscious than before, continued on. "Wouldn't you agree?" he said hoping to nicely provoke a response.

"Yes, just fantastic weather!" responded one of the officials in charge.

Dewey did not understand their silence or the long looks on their faces. The two did not seem to match but he didn't give it much more than a passing thought. He was eager to enter his food and beverage for judging. He introduced himself, "I'm Dewey Branchwhalker and I have two entries for the judges. One is a fine salad and the other a specially blended tea. I prepared both of them today and so they are very fresh."

"I'll take them here." Said the registrar, "It's very uncommon for a man to enter anything here. Usually it's the wife's job to do this."

Dewey said "Oh, well I'm not married yet and so I've been cooking for myself. I've had a bit of success with some new recipes I've developed and I'm very hopeful that the judges will like them too."

"It's just so rare, if it has even ever been done before, that a man can cook for himself let alone make something original and then bring it to be judged." responded the registrar.

Dewey felt somewhat embarrassed but since he had gotten this far he didn't want to appear any more ignorant of their customs than he already appeared. Confidently he replied "Well, as I understand it the competition is open to any one in our society, and I've been complimented on these recipes by McInnus, a very good friend of mine."

"McInnus?", she repeated, "I don't recall ever hearing that name around here before, what is his last name? Maybe I know some of his relatives."

Dewey thought quickly. If he told her his last name, Skyclimber, she would know he was a flying species and that would not go over very well at all. If he made up a name it might backfire on him and he didn't need that in this situation. "Oh, well McInnus is," he hesitantly spoke "not from around here, as a matter of fact he doesn't live on our tree or even in our grove. Anyway, all I want to do is register my entry. I'm anxious to get out and look around to see what's at this year's festival."

"Okay, you're all set, the judges will announce their decision at 1 o'clock just before the athletic competition." the registrar concluded.

Dewey was already walking away before she finished speaking He was worried something else would come up to cause him grief, "Thanks." He said as he hurried away.

Dewey wondered about visiting with old friends who he knew from cocoon class or remembered from his parent's branch where he had grown up. Most of them had taken a mate and started young families. Dewey found he had little in common with them, except that he now also owned a branch of his own. So most of what he talked with the others about had to do with agriculture and this year's crop. Everyone asked him if he had married and he got tired, very quickly, of saying no he was not married and was not planning on it any time soon. He was very comfortable with being single and did not feel that he had to be married for his life to be complete. That seemed to just get him a lot of strange looks.

Dewey met up with some of his family and was glad to see them. His parents asked him how things were going and he was happy to tell them it was going very well, but they didn't seem to be listening, just asking questions to carry a conversation. He was especially pleased to see his sister, Bev and catch up on her life, see her children and share with her about his food and nectar entries. She was very surprised to hear about it, but she encouraged Dewey anyway, as always, saying that he was smart to try to take the chance. The family stayed together in the center square of the festival and shared their lunches and visited booths close by. They tried the various foods and beverages available for sale and looked at some of the craft items made from cocoon fabric, which had been woven into quilts and fancy clothes.

One o'clock rolled around and the festival judges gathered on the pavilion platform in the very center of the square. They called for everyone's attention and announced that they were ready to award this year's winning entries for food and beverage. An elderly butterfly stood and with a loud voice called out that first place for the beverages went to Dewey's sister Bev. The crowd applauded and Bev went forward to get her blue ribbon. Second place went to Martha Weaver, who Dewey did not know. Lastly, to every one's surprise Dewey's name was called as the third place winner. A few people clapped but not for long. Dewey could hear a few people snicker in the distance. He proudly strolled up to the pavilion and got his third place ribbon and gladly shook hands with the judge who asked what his secret was. Dewey simply said, "Tell you later."

When Dewey got back to his family they all congratulated him, saying they had no idea he was so capable and what a wonderful surprise. Dewey held out hope that his food entry would also win him a ribbon but disappointments do happen and this was one of them. Dewey took it hard because he didn't like to lose and felt he had his honor to protect, especially in front of those butterflies at the registrar table. Anyway, Dewey knew the day wasn't over and hoped he would win in either the foot race or, tree climbing competition that was coming up next.

He was right, because not just to everyone else's surprise, but to his own as well, he took second place in the tree climbing competition right in front of his old best friend, Thomas, who took third. Thomas was not a very fair sport about placing behind Dewey either, he felt that anyone with the ridiculous ideas that Dewey had shared with him before certainly didn't even qualify to be in the race or at the festival. And so he told everyone that he thought might be able to do something about it, starting with the judges of the race, who, though bothered by the accusations, didn't feel they disqualified Dewey from his victory. This only angered Thomas more and so he started to tell everyone he could get to listen about Dewey's uncertainties of the butterfly's way of life and culture.

By the time Thomas got public sentiment raised high enough to get a crowd of angry butterflies to storm over to Dewey, the foot race was already poised on the starting line. As the crowd approached, they saw the race in preparation to start and booed Dewey. Then they stirred up the other onlookers to do the same, even though these newcomers had no idea at the time why they were booing and raising their fists.

PLIGHT OF THE BUTTERFLY

The starting judge raised his hand and everyone quieted down. Then he called out, "On your mark, get ready, get set, go!" And the racers took off. Dewey grunted with determination and charged forward as fast as he could. Determined not to hold back in the least, he wanted to show everyone that he could win first place and bring some credibility to his different views at the same time. He pushed feverishly with his legs, stride after stride. He pulled with his arms, racing like a gray hound dog. His entire body working in perfect union to put himself in the very front of the race. He continued to build speed that was well above any other butterfly's ability. The crowd roared with excitement and cheered him on. They were much louder than those who were still trying to boo him at his former best friend's command. Dewey ran with such high speed that most claimed they were not able to remember anyone in the past ever doing this well before. His face now clearly was showing to the crowd the great concentration of an Olympic class athlete approaching his long sought for goal line.

Dewey felt the ties of his cocoon coat loosening from the strain he was placing on them. Many of the racers had special garments they wore just for racing in, ones that gave in the joints as they moved. Dewey did not have this advantage. His coat was in poor shape from the neglect he gave it and the wear and tear from his secret training. He could hear it tearing as he ran. He feared it might break away.

He tried to imagine what might happen if it tore away. Thinking to himself, 'If I go on, I will surely win this race and vindicate myself and my choices. But if the garment comes off, I will be publicly humiliated at the same time. If I stop running I will lose certain victory and be humiliated. I will be without any excuse or defense. If my garment comes off, I will still win and have some recourse.'

And with that for reasoning, he pressed on harder to his goal line. Then his cocoon coat ripped, and half of it flew off, and was taken in the wind of his back draft.

Dewey kept right on running, even though he had nothing on. The onlooker's shock was great because there were only a few allowances in this culture for going partially dressed, like at birth and this was not one of those times. To make matters worse for Dewey, something not even he could have anticipated happened as that as his stubby wings were uncovered and began to flap in the wind, some colors other than black and brown appeared. He didn't notice this himself but the rest of the crowd did and no one cared for it either.

As if there had not already been enough surprises in this race, no one, not even Dewey was prepared for the next big one. His stubby wings, now exposed to the wind in his face and the great speed he had built up started to lift him up. He quickly realized this and made an on the spot decision that if he was going to win and vindicate himself he might as well go for it all. His eventual goal was to fly anyway and if it was going to happen now why stop? After all it was his heart's deepest longing. He was running now on only his hind pair of legs. His head and torso bobbed awkwardly up and down, like a staggering drunk at first, but he quickly managed to stay somewhat upright. Listing a little from one side and then the other, he learned to control his wings better, which were now flapping in natural motion along with the running strides he was taking.

Everyone watching was now holding their breath at such a sight. They were overwhelmed with excitement and awestruck, if not in a state of shock. Most could not believe such a thing was possible. Some would never believe, even though they were among those who were there to see it in person.

Dewey continued on in his heroic effort to fly. He bat his wings ferociously, but the physical strain on him was showing and taking its toll. He had strong muscles for walking, climbing and running, but his stubby and malformed wings could not create enough lift to hold him in flight and his muscles for flying were not at all developed for this kind of work. He, sensing his strength was going to fail soon, let out a roar that would have scared even the mocking birds away and leaped into the air in a dire attempt to fly.

At first it looked as though it were going to happen, but his nose faltered up and down a few times in the beginning and his body teetered back and forth. No one could tell if he would continue on into the skies or fall flat on his face. Then tragedy happened, he started to come down, his face revealing his fears with a look of quiet desperation. He tried in vain to run and make it a smooth landing, but he collapsed in exhaustion, rolling and toppling head over heels. He came down hard, crashing face first into a skin grinding nose dive to the ground. Dewey skid all the way until he stopped in a heap of mangled and broken pieces.

A woman screamed and broke the silence of the onlooker's tragic fright, a few started to cry and hide their faces. Then a couple of butterflies went over to see if he was still alive. Before they could get to him, he started to move. Dewey raised his head and pushed himself up with his arms shaking his head. He looked a little dizzy and dazed as though he might pass out again. When the butterflies finally got to him he was only groaning and no longer moving. They picked him up carefully and walked with him on their shoulders back to his parent's home.

What only moments ago seemed like an obtainable victory to him and for a brief passing moment to everyone else a sure thing to win the race, now ended as not only a race he lost but also as a shattered dream and public humiliation.

BUTTERFLY RENAISSANCE
CHAPTER NINE
RECOVERY
MCINNUS OFFERS TO HELP

The cocoonmum came over to Dewey's parents' house after having heard what had happened at the foot race to see how badly Dewey was injured. After seeing him, she only said, "It is hopeless. I have no idea what to do. Dewey had no business being up to this kind of thing in the first place anyway. I've brought his coat, but just look at it, he's ruined it. He obviously didn't listen in cocoon class. If your family really cared and followed our way of life, then this would never have happened. You should have watched him more closely than you did. I warned you! Just look at this coat, it's been neglected and is ruined from having been taken in the wind. Now it's worthless. He is finished. I don't think he can even walk any more." With that she simply stormed out of their house and went back to the festival. Dewey's family was very displeased with her... her lack of abilities in this crisis for such a self acclaimed person and her shaming words. Dewey's father had no idea what to do.

Things did not end there though. Dewey's friend McInnus seemed to have a way of showing up when he was needed and this could not have been better timing. When McInnus arrived he was a welcomed sight. The family knew of him from the past and Dewey had continued to mention his name on rare occasions. McInnus introduced himself to Dewey's parents with great respect, saying he had heard of the accident and hoped he could see Dewey for a moment. He tried to encourage Dewey without giving him false hope, then he suggested to his friend that he should rest.

With that he went out to see Dewey's parents. McInnus wanted to offer the help of his community's hospital, but was very unsure about the best way to bring it up without alienating himself from Dewey's family. To his surprise and relief, Dewey's parents asked him about it first.

"We've heard, though we don't know if it is true, that you have in your community a place for people who are sick or injured to go. A place where they can get the help they need so that they can get well and recover. Is this true?"

McInnus replied, "Yes, I was wanting to bring it up, but I was not sure how you would feel about it. Our two cultures differ in so many ways. It's a hospital with many people who are trained and gifted in healing and recovery arts. I would like to bring Dewey there."

"We are glad that this is true. Normally our own cocoonmums would be able to offer help with problems similar to this. But she has come and gone leaving us with no hope." said Dewey's father.

McInnus offered, "Well, then let me go to my community and ask them for help. If they are agreeable, I will return early tomorrow to take Dewey there."

"Good, we have no idea of what else to do. This is our only hope," sighed Dewey's father.

McInnus returned the next morning about an hour after sunrise. With him came four large, more mature butterflies, who were not very talkative but were always polite and respectful. McInnus said that they would be using a large, fresh rhubarb leaf, which they brought with, to carry Dewey on.

Two of the butterflies carefully lifted Dewey from his bed and ever so gently placed him in the center of the leaf. Then together the four of them carried Dewey to an open area on the branch. For a moment they let the sun warm their wings and muscles. Then, in harmony, they spread their wings and lifted Dewey into the air as they flew away with him. McInnus stayed with Dewey's family for another moment. He shared with Dewey's parents that he would visit Dewey in the hospital to encourage him and see how he was doing.

When Dewey arrived at the community hospital he was taken to a treatment room. There he was amazed to see how large and fresh looking it was. It was unlike the cocoon houses he had been in. The ceiling was raised so high, he thought maybe as many as twenty butterflies could stand on each other's shoulders before they reached to the top.

He was not alone in this room, there were many other butterflies there. They all were of the flying species. They were lined up together in a row and the staff would come and get them to bring them to various parts of the room for their treatment. He couldn't see everything going on there, but he could see equipment that was new to him, designed for exercise and strengthening. There were also many curtains that kept his curious mind from seeing in.

Before long, a butterfly came over to him and introduced herself as Chrys, saying "I'm your therapist and today I'm going to start by doing an assessment of your current state. We're on our way now to a table." As she began to push Dewey on his stretcher. She added, "We will lift you onto the table. It's padded and it will be a little more comfortable for you with what we have to do."

When they approached the table another helper arrived. Together they lifted Dewey with care and set him gently down. Chrys explained to him that she would begin by measuring the mobility of his joints in his legs, arms and wings.

"This," she said, "will definitely make you uncomfortable. But you need to tell me first when it begins to be uncomfortable, then when it starts to hurt. But allow me to move the joint to the point where the pain is so bad that you need me to stop. After we are done you can get settled in the room you will be staying in while you're here."

With that she systematically proceeded with testing each leg, arm and wing, moving them slowly in all directions. Her helper sat with pen and paper in hand and wrote down whatever Chrys said to him. She would state which limb it was and which side of the body it was on. Then she would move the joint outward, telling him the angle of flexion when she first met resistance, or his first sensation of pain and where the pain was so bad that he wanted her to stop. Chrys would call out the angle again, and the helper would write it down.

When they were done, Dewey was tired out and asked if he could be brought to his room and get settled in for a rest. Chrys agreed and spoke encouraging words to Dewey, stating he had done a great job at an unpleasant task without complaining even once. She and the helper lifted Dewey carefully to the stretcher and then they pushed him to his room. On the way there she explained that they would meet with him again in the afternoon. Then she would go over the results of the morning's assessment and explain to him the plan they would use to help him get better. Dewey was glad to hear this because he felt very much in the dark about what was going on and what to expect.

After lunch Dewey returned to physical therapy and met with Chrys who shared with him her plan for his recovery from his injuries. She promised that he would be able to fly when he was done. She shared how his stunted wings would be softened with warm whirlpool baths and stretched fully open. Then how his wings muscles would be strengthened with increasingly more difficult exercises. Dewey wasn't sure he understood what all this meant or how it would happen, but he was willing to try.

His first stop was at the whirlpool. He slowly got into the water which was very warm and relaxing. Then the whirlpool was started up, sending waves of bubbles and hot water across Dewey. When it was done, he felt very tired and drained. As he climbed out, he felt and looked like a dripping limp leaf bud.

Next Chrys joined him and together they stretched out Dewey's wings. She held Dewey firmly and pulled gently to the point where the tension was just tolerable but not without some pain. She took his wings, opening them and spreading them as far open as they would go, which was only about one quarter of the fullness of her wings. Then she asked Dewey to work on this exercise on his own until she came back. Dewey struggled to open his wings and found that not only were his stubby wings stiff, but also they were weak. He worked hard at it until he no longer had the strength to go on. Chrys soon returned and encouraged Dewey that he had done well his first day. She added that not only would the work get tougher, but that he would also grow more flexible and stronger each day because of it.

REUNION WITH COURTLYNN

After the afternoon session Dewey returned to his room to see he had a visitor. She was a petite butterfly with a beautiful smile.

She spoke first, "Dewey, I'm Courtlynn. You remember?"

Dewey remembered, but what he remembered of Courtlynn was that she was an irritating caterpillar who didn't fit in very well back on his old tree.

He shook his head, not knowing what to say, "Are you the Courtlynn I knew from before?"

"Yes, of course, only now I'm a butterfly."

Dewey still did not know what to say. He had no idea how she came to be a flying butterfly or how to politely ask her. Lucky for him she could tell he had questions.

"Dewey, I know you must be wondering what I'm doing here and why I'm a flying butterfly. When the time came for me to spin my cocoon I hid from my family and choose to not get help from a cocoonmum. I really didn't believe what I was taught in cocoon class. I decided to do things differently, especially after I overheard about you seeing a flying species butterfly break out of his cocoon on his own. I felt I had nothing to loose. I broke free of my cocoon and when I was done, I could fly."

Dewey didn't remember Courtlynn ever spinning a cocoon, seeing her as a flying butterfly or even hearing anything about her disappearing. He was unbelieving, but seeing her was hard to deny.

He asked her, "So what did you do then?"

She answered, "I left the tree we grew up on and now I am probably considered one of those butterflies who was 'never heard of again'."

Dewey sat in silence for a while and then spoke, "I'm amazed. I don't understand all that has gone on in my life, although I'm working on it. I'm getting a lot of help here, but they also make me do a lot of the work. My goal is to be able to fly like you. Only thing is, I can't spin another cocoon to break free of because it's too late in my life for that. That much I understand. My physical therapist, Chrys, is helping me. She's is very confident that I will be able to fly soon."

"Dewey, I'm very glad you're here and working on your goal. I'm sure, with the right help from Chrys and enough hard work on your part, you will fly."

Dewey was looking more and more drowsy as they spoke. So Courtlynn politely said, "I know that you are tired and so you should get your rest. I hope to see you again. Bye Dewey."

"Courtlynn, I hope to see you again too." said Dewey.

DAY TWO

As Dewey woke the next morning he felt especially tired and groggy. He reached with his limbs to stretch. Instead he was stopped by shooting pains that the stretching had triggered. His joints were extremely tight and his muscles burned deep to the center of his body. This pain was more intense than when he crashed at the race only two days before. Why should he 'feel worse and not better' he thought? He moved more slowly and decided to ask Chrys about his pain later.

Dewey went to his morning therapy session and there he and Chrys started work on his recovery again. "Dewey, this morning we're going to start some strengthening exercises," said Chrys as the therapy session began.

Dewey objected saying, "Chrys, I'm already strong and fast too. In our midsummer festival, back home on my tree, I took second place in the tree climbing race. I was also going to be first in the foot race, before I crashed. As a matter of fact, I was almost flying I was running so fast. I think I'm already very strong. Only this morning I felt a lot of pain, why was that?"

"Dewey, I'm sure that is all true. But the muscles you use for running and climbing are not the same ones used for flying. Those muscles are still under developed and weak. The pain you felt was because you are stunted and inflexible. We are stretching you out and these changes are uncomfortable. As for flying, I'm sure with your wing muscles as weak as they are, you quickly became tired when you tried to fly. Your wings also are stunted, making them too small to lift you anywhere. It didn't matter how hard you tried, you weren't going to fly, no matter what you did."

Dewey was silent for a moment. Tears welled up in his eyes and he turned away as he wiped them from his face. "I've tried to fly, more than once. I got my friend McInnus to help lift me into the air, but it didn't work. Then I built a flying craft with feathers and tried to fly with it, but it spiraled into the ground and crashed. In the foot race my cocoon coat tore and was ripped off me, then it flew away in the wind. I thought I could fly then. I was barely up in the air and then I just tumbled to the ground and was badly injured.

"I don't understand why I haven't been able to fly. All my efforts failed. Why would things be different now? If it didn't matter what I tried then, why am I going to be doing all this work now any way?"

Chrys responded, "It won't be long and you will fly. You must believe in me. Your wings will expand with stretching and your muscles will grow strong from exercise. You will work it out, but you must have my help. That will make the difference."

As they worked together at stretching, Chrys told Dewey, "If you relax and concentrate hard not to resist, it will hurt less. You will find that, as we start the stretching, your first natural reflex is to tighten up. After that happens you can consciously relax your muscles. You will see how they will stretch farther as you let me help you. Trust me, I won't go farther than you let me."

After the morning session Dewey went for lunch and then returned to therapy for the afternoon. He was still tired and sore from the morning workout and couldn't do much because his muscles were cramping a lot. Still, he did work as hard as he was able. It was discouraging to Dewey to not make as much progress as he would have liked.

Chrys encouraged him saying "You can't always have a better session than the previous one. The reality of it is that everybody gets tired out occasionally." With that said, Chrys worked more on stretching and less on strengthening, knowing that this would help Dewey's cramping muscles to relax.

REUNION WITH ED

That evening Dewey sat in a lounge outside the dinning room and enjoyed the cool evening breeze. He relaxed and looked forward to a good night's rest.

Soon a large and strong butterfly came over to him and said, "Hi Dewey, how are you? It's been a long time, hasn't it?"

Dewey did not know this butterfly, not that he remembered anyway. He found everyone so friendly that it was hard not to forget one or two acquaintances along the way.

Dewey returned the greeting, "Hi, you look familiar but I'm afraid I'm don't remember where we first met."

"Dewey, we met a long, long time ago. We grew up together as caterpillars. I'm your brother Ed!"

"Ed, you're alive?" Dewey said as tears started to stream down his face, "But, but the cocoonmum said that you had died in the storm while you were in your cocoon." The two of them hugged and cried. Then Dewey spoke again, "Ed, I missed you so much, tell me what happened that night?"

"After the storm passed, I woke and I didn't call for help. I had waited for a night when I believed it would rain. That way I could break out of my cocoon by myself. I knew that if I did that, I would be able to fly. If I let a cocoonmum cut me out then I would have been destined to spend the rest of my life on that tree, flightless and wearing a cocoon coat. I couldn't do that, I needed to leave. So I broke out and let my wings dry in the early morning sun."

Dewey sat in silence for a moment, not knowing what to think of Ed's words. Then he spoke, "I'm going to have to spend some time thinking about this. It is all so different here from what I was taught."

Dewey and Ed stayed and talked for a long time about growing up together and what life had been like after the night of the storm. Dewey eventually tired first and needed to say good night. So they agreed to spend more time together later, after Dewey had more time to heal from his accident.

DAY THREE

In the morning Dewey arrived in therapy and started his whirlpool bath. The warm jets of water helped him to waken and loosen up. His muscles were always stiff and sore from the previous day's workout.

After this he went to the exercise room, where Chrys set out to help Dewey with his exercises. She systematically worked each leg, arm and wing. First stretching, then exercising for strength and then again stretching each limb. She gently pulled each limb out to its maximum extension and held it open for a minute or two. Then she would have Dewey push against her as she applied resistance, helping him to slowly extend and build his strength. This was repeated over and over until Dewey observed how his stunted wings were beginning to unfold just like a little leaf or flower blossom would open.

That evening, Dewey quietly lay on his bed, physically tired from his workout but mentally alert. What wasn't hurting from stretching was hurting from the strengthening exercises. He felt too sore and tired to move but was still wide awake. As he relaxed he became aware of his feelings coming to the surface and forming with clarity, not remaining vague like in his youth.

He felt anger for not having learned the truth about Ed until now. The cocoonmum must have known or at least had a suspicion. She must have suppressed the possibility that Ed broke out and flew away and instead pushed her strong opinions on everyone. 'Why,' Dewey thought, 'Couldn't I have figured these things out for myself? Ed must have. Courtlynn too, must have been able to figure this out for herself.' What was it that he was missing?

Dewey thought back to his cocoon birthing and how he had waited for the cocoonmum to help him out after he woke up, just as he was taught. He searched his mind for the details but found he was unable to draw anything out.

What was it that he was missing he thought to himself? He had such a detailed mind, how could he have forgotten this time in his life? He felt anger again, anger that grew from what had seemed like a small matter to where now he felt he might explode.

He didn't remember calling for help. He didn't remember because it never happened that way. He remembered how he woke up after it was all over. He had no chance to break out of his cocoon, even if he had wanted to.

Dewey yelled out, "NO...! NO...! Why?" He wept as he pondered that day over in his mind. He felt as though someone had pulled the rug out from under his feet. The cocoonmums had taught that it would be less than instinctive to call out for help, yet Dewey wasn't even given the chance to do that much. She said that it would be instinctive to wiggle, like McInnus had done as he worked so hard to break free of his cocoon, but he was not to embarrass the family and wiggle like a worm. As a matter of fact all the flightless butterflies resembled worms with legs and a lot like the caterpillars they started out as.

Some of this was starting to fit together for Dewey. It reminded him of a childhood wish, that some day all that he had learned would somehow fit into one large consistent picture. Now, for him, that picture was finally starting to take shape. Dewey wiped away the tears that had slowly fallen down his face. He was saddened by his upbringing, but now he also felt like he had hope.

He believed the help Chrys was giving him would turn his life around. Knowing now that he could see the changes taking place day by day gave him encouragement. While he had tense times to go through, Dewey felt more at peace now than the day before. He rolled over, relaxed, sighed deeply and fell off to sleep.

DEWEY'S DREAM

Dewey woke in a startle, out of breath and ready to scream in fear but couldn't. He stopped and looked around the darkened room. His heart was racing and he felt frightened. He sat in bed and pondered what it was that had woken him with such a start. He looked around the room and could see he was in no danger. Then it came to him as he relaxed, it was a dream.

Unlike before when he could not remember his dreams, this one returned to him. He was back on his branch, but there was a river running next to him too. He had gone over to the river to sip some water. Suddenly the current swept him off his feet and he fell in. The water quickly soaked him and his cocoon coat thoroughly. He tried to swim but the weight of his body and wet cocoon coat were too much. It drew him under and he feared he would drown.

The rushing water had twisted his body into a tangled mass as it swiftly swept him about. He was dizzy and hungry for air. The more he struggled the more he sank. He thought that if he could only take off his cocoon coat he could swim. He struggled and fought to remove it as fast as possible, but he was quickly exhausted and nearly passed into unconsciousness as it finally came off.

Fully exhausted he gave up trying to swim and gave into what he thought would be his death. Before he passed out an air bubble surrounded him. He could breathe in there but he was still exhausted and unable to move. The bubble he was in floated slowly to the surface of the river and then effortlessly took him up into the air and far away from his tree. He thought to himself, 'This must be what it is like for a butterfly to fly, or maybe this is what it is like when you die'. It was then that the bubble popped and he suddenly woke in fear.

Dewey did not feel afraid any more. He felt like this dream was good for him, that it was a promise of what he had achieved so far in his life. Dewey laid down again and returned to sleep, knowing that he needed to get his rest. Tomorrow he wanted to talk to Chrys about many of his thoughts and work hard on his recovery.

MIDWAY

The next day was Wednesday and Chrys set out to reevaluate Dewey's progress. They began by measuring the flexibility of his wings and the comfort level he experienced. Chrys also started to measure the strength of Dewey's wing muscles.

Then she shared what she found, "Dewey, you're progressing on your recovery nicely. Your flexibility is up to sixty percent of normal, but the pain level remains the same at the point of maximum extension. Your strength is up to about sixty percent of normal now too.   However, I have to believe that your endurance is not developed very well yet.   We will keep doing these same exercises for strengthening, stretching for your flexibility and whirlpool baths too."

"Chrys," said Dewey, "Over the past few days after therapy my brother visited me and so did an old friend. I don't ever see you outside of therapy. Why don't we spend time talking or eating together?"

To which Chrys replied, "Where I am going you may not yet come, but when you have healed and learned to fly then you may come."

"Chrys," Dewey said, "I need to run some things past you that I've been thinking about."

"OKAY" Chrys said, "We have time for that."

"What really has been bothering me is that nobody told me the truth about life back on my tree. They eat that old stale food when there is plenty of fresh. They wear cocoons instead of break out of them and they push their lifestyle on others. They wrap themselves up in that stage of life, never maturing out of it. They have stagnated at the part of life when they could have changed for the better. Isn't that all true?"

Chrys was silent for just a moment and then thoughtfully answered Dewey, "You're right Dewey, that's all true. So what do you want now that you can choose between your old life and a new one?"

"I don't even need to think about that. I don't want to go back to that old life. But I cannot go back and make another cocoon to break out of, to start a new life like a butterfly should be able to do. That stage of my life is over. My cocoon was cut open and I was removed from the struggle that would have freed me from that stage in life. So where does that leave me?"

"Breaking," Chrys responded, "out of the cocoon is the way you move into the next cycle of life. It is a struggle, but you must travail and work through it. You were not allowed to do this."

"But in many ways, you have already broken out of your cocoon. You challenged with your mind what you thought was wrong and you came up with the right answers. When your cocoon coat tore in the race and ripped off you, it was almost the same as if you broke out of it. The missing parts of your changing into a butterfly are the last of the physical and emotional struggles we all must go through in becoming free of the cocoon. You are no longer wearing yours and before the week is over, you will be flying as a butterfly should."

"Chrys, it's hard to know that they taught me the wrong things and not to hate them for it. What do I do with the hate? Those cocoonmums are all alike, they think they are high and mighty. They cannot do what only I can do for myself and they cannot replace my cocoon." Dewey said.

"You cannot go back in time and remake the past, but you can live in it. Hate locks on to a butterfly and keeps you from flying, it stops you from changing with an ongoing life. To put hate aside, you need to release those who did you wrong from what they did." said Chrys.

A VISIT FROM MCINNUS

The day was soon coming to an end and in the evening Dewey's long time friend, McInnus, came to visit. Dewey was relaxed as he spoke with his friend. "It has been a very intense week, McInnus. When I came here I had no idea what it would be like. Things are so different."

To which McInnus said, "So you're finding out what life is like on a different tree? I'm glad that you're here and getting help. Your life back on your old tree, although by those standards was good and successful, cannot compare to life here. Chrys told me you're doing well and making great progress."

"I've had to work harder than I've ever worked before, but in a different way. Things aren't just handed to me like my inheritance of cocoon fabric and food stores were. I'm also finding out the truth about different things, like my brother's disappearance." said Dewey.

McInnus replied, "I'm very glad for you Dewey. We've been friends ever since we first met. Soon we will meet in the skies and fly together."

"I'm looking forward to that McInnus." said Dewey.

"I can see that you're getting tired and I know that you have much work ahead of you tomorrow. I will let you get to bed. Good-bye Dewey." said McInnus as he left. "Good night McInnus." Said Dewey as he went to bed.

The next day was Thursday and in the afternoon Dewey finally asked Chrys about the pain he had been having all week and why it went so deep. While it was better, he still was not sure of its role in his recovery. Because he had been sheltered from uncomfortable events in his life by his family and the cocoonmum, he didn't understand how pain occurred or why.

Chrys explained, "The deep pain is just that Dewey. You feel sore because of the changes that are going on. When a caterpillar becomes a butterfly, it is not only on the surface that you change. It's more than just wings that sprout out and antennas that unfold. The internal organs of a butterfly are changed from those of the caterpillar. As you stretch your wings out, it's not just the expanding of the wings that you are experiencing. Because they are unfolding from your innermost being as they expand, they are pulling to rearrange your internal organs. In the short time you spent in your cocoon those changes only started, but they never were completed. The water in the cocoon eases and washes away the old you, which sloughs off in the water bath. It soaks in and soothes you.

"The cocoon is a place of security, you felt that as you fell asleep. The compactness of the cocoon applies stress and focus. Breaking out is a struggle as you travail in labor against its resistance. To have stayed in the cocoon longer would have allowed the changes to take place.

Then, breaking out of the cocoon, your wings would have opened and you would have completed the changes. Warmth from the sun drying your wings would have solidified the changes.

"When the cocoonmum cut open your cocoon, pulled you out and dried you off, this process all stopped instantly. Some of this pain you've had the past few days, you would have experienced even if you had broken out of your cocoon. However, it would have been less intense and more tolerable. No life is without problems. Because your change to a butterfly is later in life and without the benefit of your cocoon, the way life was designed to be, the pain is greater. You have been doing your part and I have done everything I can for you."

After this talk with Chrys, Dewey worked extremely hard to reach his goal, enduring the difficulties and facing the struggle straight on. Unlike what he was taught as a youth in the cocoon class, Dewey choose now to endure the intense struggle. He grew stronger and increased in flexibility. His wings slowly continued to open more fully. He was building the enduring strength he would need to support and move them.

BUTTERFLY RENAISSANCE
CHAPTER TEN
FLIGHT OF THE BUTTERFLY

Dewey had no idea what he was in for that next afternoon when he went out to the patio for a sun bath. He was feeling very good about his progress and wondered why he wasn't taken for a morning workout in physical therapy. He sat outstretched in a soft comfortable lounge chair. Looking at his legs he wondered if he would ever do anything more than just stand and take a few unsteady steps. He stretched in the warmth of the sun and felt his body's new flexibility, especially in his wings. They expanded now more than ever and without the pain he once knew.

His physical therapist, Chrys, came over and sat next to him. She was looking excited and jubilant.

"Dewey, how are you feeling today?" she asked.

Dewey said "Better than ever, but I was surprised you gave me the morning off. I'm not wanting to slow down in my recovery."

"You're not slowing down, not at all. We're ready to start a new phase in your therapy. I'm sure you will be as happy about it as I am. Every time I see a patient get to this point in their recovery, it is a new adventure in excitement for me."

Dewey wondered what she was talking about, "OKAY, so are you going to tell me what new kind of therapy you're going to give me now?"

"All right," she said, "today you are finally going to fly!"

Dewey just sat there dumbfounded for a moment. He was thinking how comfortable he had been up to this point in the day and that as he faced his time to take to flight, he was afraid. Up to now, every time he had attempted to fly it was by his choosing, his plan, and his way. Now he had to get used to the idea in a whole new light. He wasn't choosing when, or how. It was being done for him and he felt a little frightened.

"Chrys, what must I do?" he asked. If this is the real thing, he was not going to miss out, even if it meant doing things other than his own way. He did not want doubts or insecurities to overcome him. He wanted only to trust and have faith because of the hard work he and Chrys done together.

The time had come and the elements were in place for his goal to be reached and that was without a doubt. Chrys walked over to the edge of the creek that watered their tree and looking Dewey right in the eyes said gently, "Stand here, next to me." This Dewey did without delay.

One of the therapy assistants also came to help. Then Chrys said "We are going to use the creek today. We are going to lift you into the water completely.

Your entire body will be going under. Then we will take you out and you will climb the tree with me and hang there while your wings are pulled open by the weight of the water and dry in the warmth of the sun."

Dewey felt comfortable with everything she said up to the point where she said he would be going completely under water. Dewey had only dreamt of this before and was not at all sure whether this was what it was like to fly or what it was like to die. But he silently agreed and nodded his head. Chrys and her helper lifted Dewey up and took him into the water together. There they gently held him and slowly lowered him down into the water until he was completely under, antenna and all. Then they lifted him up and walked with him up to the side of the creek and let Dewey stand.

Dewey spoke out, "That was really something! It was much more intense than the whirlpool, especially when my head and antenna went under."

Chrys looked toward Dewey and said that this was what everyone experienced at this point in their recovery. She climbed the tree that was next to the creek and invited Dewey to also, saying that they must hang on the tree for their wings to dry correctly. Then she opened her wings in a show of beauty that Dewey had never seen before. It was as though a film of dirt had been washed away from his eyes in the creek's water.

Chrys said, "Dewey, climb the tree and hang like me. This is how my wings look when they are wet. If you open yours up now, you too will see something magnificent about yourself."

Dewey was in awe at the greatness and glory of Chrys' wings. He was unable to talk, but in kind of an automated response to the trust and faith he had in Chrys, he did what she asked without even giving it so much as a second thought. Dewey turned his head to the right and then to the left. He felt new and different, like he was looking at someone else, but he knew it was himself that he saw. It was hard to believe but still it was more than undeniable. He was very pleased he had done what Chrys had asked.

Chrys, having given him a little bit of time to get used to his new image, turned her wings into the sun, and said, "Dewey, turn your wings into the sun too."

This he did, still in silent awe. In a few moments, the water had dripped off and evaporated from both of their bodies. Now, for the first time ever, Dewey could stretch out his wings completely and without pain too. He felt so happy!

As the last drop of water fell from his body and the sun's warmth overwhelmed him, he felt tingles of renewing strength spread throughout his body. The sun warmed his wings and they started to move rhythmically, with every heart beat. Then in an instant, something happened which took Dewey to another new height of wonder. Chrys' wings began to shine like the sun, flickering on and off once or twice for the briefest of moments. Dewey saw in them a great intensity that was bold and blinding.

Then another flash of light came from behind, beside and over his head. As he turned to look, he could scarcely believe it, but it was happening before his very own eyes. His wings began to flicker on and off, as lightening in the nighttime, giving off intense light too. Then the flashing stopped, but his wings continued to glow with warm heat. They were colored in metallic green and blue with silver. The colors moved about on his wings like a gently flowing stream and he felt empowered like never before.

Chrys, looking into the distance started to gently sweep her wings and then said, "Let's go for a flight!"

Dewey, unquestioningly swept his wings back and forth and followed her into the air. What he had tried to do before, in many different ways and had failed, now was happening. Together they rose in flight and took to the skies.

Soon Chrys turned to Dewey and spoke to him, "Your name should not be Dewey Branchwhalker anymore, from the dew on your brow as your father found you that one day. Your name is now Chrystopher Windjammer, because now you can fly on the winds of the air."

With a newfound joy, this once confused young butterfly, flew through the summer skies eager to explore the world beyond. The sheer delight and joy of the moment was the beginning of a new, exciting life for Chrystopher Windjammer.

THE END